DISCOVERING AMERICA

South Central

ARKANSAS • KANSAS • LOUISIANA • MISSOURI • OKLAHOMA

By
Thomas G. Aylesworth
Virginia L. Aylesworth

CHELSEA HOUSE PUBLISHERS
New York • Philadelphia

3   5   7   9   8   6   4   2

Library of Congress Cataloging-in-Publication Data

Aylesworth, Thomas G.
    South Central: Arkansas, Kansas, Louisiana, Missouri, Oklahoma
Thomas G. Aylesworth, Virginia L. Aylesworth.
        p. cm.—(Discovering America)
    Includes bibliographical references and index.
    ISBN 0-7910-3410-0.
        0-7910-3428-3 (pbk.)
    1. Southwestern States—Juvenile literature. I. Aylesworth, Virginia L. II. Title. III. Series.

F396.A95   1995   94-42010
979—dc20   CIP
                                            AC

CONTENTS

Arkansas

The state seal of Arkansas, adopted in 1864, is circular. At the bottom is a shield bearing pictures of a steamboat, plow and beehive, and a sheaf of wheat. These stand for the state's industry and agriculture. To the left of the shield is the Angel of Mercy holding a banner on which is printed "Mercy," and to the right is the sword of justice bearing the word "Justice." Behind the shield is an American eagle carrying a banner inscribed with the state motto. Above the eagle is the Goddess of Liberty surrounded by thirteen stars. Around the circle is printed "Great Seal of the State of Arkansas."

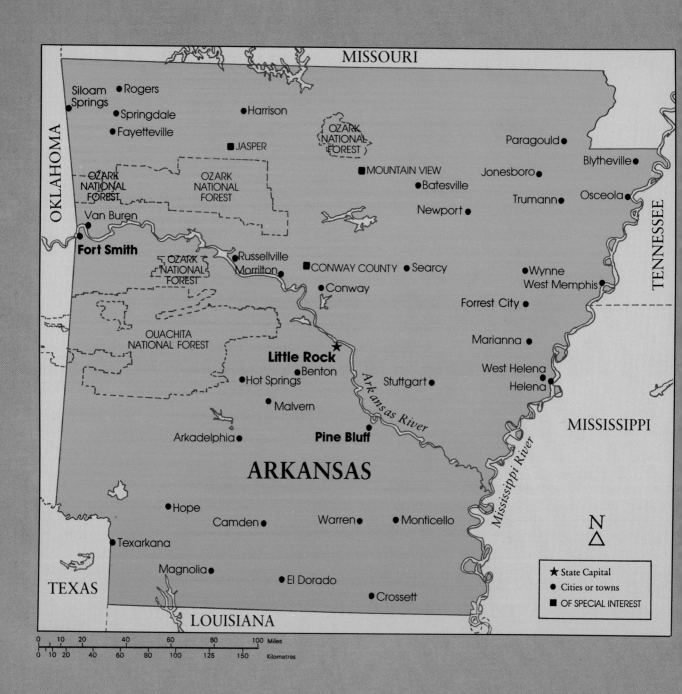

MISSOURI

OKLAHOMA

Siloam Springs • Rogers
• Springdale • Harrison
• Fayetteville
■ JASPER
OZARK NATIONAL FOREST
■ MOUNTAIN VIEW
OZARK NATIONAL FOREST
OZARK NATIONAL FOREST
• Batesville
Van Buren
• Newport
Fort Smith
OZARK NATIONAL FOREST
• Russellville
• Morrilton
■ CONWAY COUNTY • Searcy
• Conway
OUACHITA NATIONAL FOREST
Little Rock ★
• Benton
Arkansas River
• Hot Springs
Stuttgart •
• Malvern

ARKANSAS

Arkadelphia •
Pine Bluff

Paragould •
Blytheville •
Jonesboro •
Trumann • Osceola •

TENNESSEE

• Wynne
West Memphis •
Forrest City •
Marianna •
West Helena •
Helena ■

MISSISSIPPI

Mississippi River

• Hope
Camden • Warren • • Monticello
N
△
• Texarkana
Magnolia •
• El Dorado
• Crossett

★ State Capital
• Cities or towns
■ OF SPECIAL INTEREST

TEXAS

LOUISIANA

| 0 | 10 | 20 | 40 | 60 | 80 | 100 Miles |
| 0 | 10 | 20 | 40 | 60 | 80 | 100 | 125 | 150 Kilometres |

ARKANSAS
At a Glance

State Flag

Capital: Little Rock

Major Industries: Aluminum, fertilizer, forest products, livestock

Major Crops: Soybeans, rice, cotton, hay

State Flower:
Apple Blossom

State Bird:
Mockingbird

Size: 53,187 square miles (27th largest)
Population: 2,398,767 (33rd largest)

State Flag

The state flag was adopted in 1913 and amended in 1923. A large white diamond, symbolizing Arkansas' status as the only diamond-producing state, is surrounded by 25 stars on a blue border inside a field of red. Inside the diamond is inscribed "Arkansas" and four stars, standing for the four nations whose flags have flown over Arkansas—France, Spain, the Confederate States of America, and the United States of America.

State Motto

Regnat Populus

This motto, Latin for "The people rule," was adopted in 1907.

Hikers enjoy the scenery of the Buffalo National River, where private citizens live and farm in the valley under an agreement with the National Park Service.

State Name and Nicknames

The name Arkansas was first recorded by Father Jacques Marquette in 1673. He took it from the Kansa Indians, who used it to mean "downstream people."

The official nickname of the state is the *Land of Opportunity*. It has also been referred to as the *Bowie State*, after the famous knife made for Jim Bowie. Another nickname is the *Hot Water State* because of the hot springs that can be found there.

State Flower

In 1901, Arkansas selected the apple blossom, *Pyrus malus*, as the state flower.

State Tree

The pine, *Pinus palustris*, was named state tree of Arkansas in 1939.

State Bird

The State Federation of Women's Clubs convinced the state legislature to select the mockingbird, *Mimus polyglottos*, as state bird in 1929.

State Beverage

Milk was named state beverage in 1985.

State Gem

The diamond was adopted state gem in 1967.

State Insect

The honeybee, *Apis mellifera*, became the state insect in 1973.

State Mineral

Adopted in 1967, the state mineral is the quartz crystal.

State Musical Instrument

The fiddle has been the state musical instrument since 1985.

State Rock

Bauxite, an aluminum ore, was designated state rock in 1967.

State Song

Adopted by the legislature in 1917, the state song is "Arkansas," by Eva Ware Barnett.

State Capital

Little Rock has always been the capital city.

Population

The population of Arkansas in 1992 was 2,398,767, making it the 33rd most populous state. There are 44.2 people per square mile.

Industries

The principal industries of Arkansas are agriculture, tourism, and forestry. The chief manufactured products are lumber, paper, food products, home appliances, chemicals, electric motors, furniture, garments, machinery, auto and airplane parts, and petroleum products.

Agriculture

The chief crops of the state are soybeans, rice, cotton, watermelons, wine grapes, blueberries, and apples. Arkansas is also a livestock state, and there are estimated to be some 1.71 million cattle, 760,000 hogs and pigs, and 980 million poultry

The waterfalls in the Ozark National Forest.

on its farms. Oak, hickory, gum, cypress, and pine trees are harvested. Abrasives, bauxite, and bromine are important mineral resources.

Government

The governor of Arkansas is elected to a four-year term, as are the lieutenant governor, secretary of state, attorney general, treasurer, auditor, and land commissioner. The state legislature, or general assembly, which meets in odd-numbered years, consists of a 35-member senate and a 100-member house of representatives. Senators are elected by senatorial districts and serve four-year terms. Representatives are elected from representative districts and serve two-year terms. The most recent state constitution was adopted in 1874. In addition to its two U.S. senators, Arkansas has four representatives in the House of Representatives. The state has six votes in the electoral college.

Sports

Arkansas is a sports state, especially when it comes to football. The University of Arkansas has won many post-season bowls including the Orange Bowl, the Sugar Bowl, and the Cotton Bowl.

Major Cities

Fort Smith (population 72,798). The first settler, John Rogers, arrived in 1822. The town grew up around the fort, which was built in 1817. By 1842, the town had a population of nearly 500. It became a supply center for gold-rush wagons heading for California in 1848. A lawless town, it was not cleaned up until 1875. Today it is a leading manufacturing city, home to more than 200 industrial plants. Fort Smith has rich agricultural lands, and coal, gas, and timber are all plentiful.

Things to see in Fort Smith: Little Theatre, Fort Smith Art Center, over 900 acres of parks with fishing in the lakes and streams and game for hunters in prairies and woodland.

Hot Springs (population 32,462). Set aside as a federal reservation in 1832 and incorporated in 1851, this city adjoins Hot Springs National Park, established in 1921. The park covers 1,016 acres of forest, mountains, streams, and level terrain. There are 47 springs in the area, yielding a daily flow of one million gallons of water. Bottled spring water from the hot springs is sold throughout the United States. Millions of tourists visit to drink the water and enjoy the thermal baths. Native Americans utilized the healing properties of this water long before Europeans arrived.

Hot Springs and its surrounding areas are also rich in minerals. Approximately 75 different types of minerals have been identified at Magnet Cove near Hot Springs, and the nation's only diamond field was first discovered near Murfreesboro by farmer John M. Huddleston in 1906 and has yielded gems worth up to $250,000.

Things to see in Hot Springs: Fine arts center; Hamilton, Catherine, and Ouachita lakes; and numerous hiking and horseback riding trails.

Little Rock (population 175,727). Settled in 1812, the capital city is the center for transportation, education, culture, and government. The most populous city in the state, its name came from French explorers who called this site on the Arkansas

The Ozark Folk Center, in Mountain View, celebrates the cultural heritage of rural Arkansas with native crafts, folk and harvest festivals, and banjo, guitar, and fiddle contests.

River "La Petite Roche." The nation's largest supply of bauxite is mined near the outskirts of Little Rock, and much of the surrounding area is farmland whose principal products are cotton and soybeans.

Things to see in Little Rock:
State Capitol, Old State House, Arkansas Territorial Restoration, Arkansas Museum of Science and History, Decorative Arts Museum, Old Mill (1828), Little Rock Zoo, MacArthur Park—including the birthplace of General Douglas MacArthur and the Arkansas Art Center.

Pine Bluff (population 57,140). Founded in 1819, Pine Bluff was occupied by Union troops in 1863 and remained in Union hands until the end of the Civil War. Today it is an industrial city surrounded by vast recreation areas.

Things to see in Pine Bluff:
Jefferson County Historical Museum, and Dexter Harding House.

Places to Visit

The National Park Service maintains eight areas in the state of Arkansas: Arkansas Post National Memorial, Buffalo National River, Fort Smith National Historic Site, Hot Springs National Park, Pea Ridge National Military Park, Ouachita National Forest, Ozark National Forest, and St. Francis National Forest. In addition, there are 28 state recreation areas.

Berryville: Cosmic Cavern. The cavern is Arkansas' largest underground lake.
Bull Shoals Lake: Mountain Village 1890. An Ozark village with authentic buildings, including a bank and general store.
Hot Springs: Tiny Town. This is an indoor mechanical village.
Mountain View: Ozark Folk Center State Park. Fifty old buildings are located in this 915-acre site.

Events

There are many events and organizations that schedule activities of various kinds in the state of Arkansas. Here are some of them.

Sports: National Explorer Canoe Race (Batesville), Arkansas All Arabian Horse Show (Little Rock), Riverboat Days and State Catfish Cooking

The skyline of Little Rock.

Contest (Newport), World Championship Duck Calling Contest (Stuttgart).
Arts and Crafts: Festival of the Two Rivers (Arkadelphia), Jonquil Festival (Hope).
Music: Ozark Folk Festival (Eureka Springs), Warfield Concert Series (Helena), Arkansas Symphony (Little Rock), Arkansas Folk Festival (Mountain View), Arkansas State Fiddler's Contest (Mountain View), Gospel Festival (Springdale).
Entertainment: Arkansas-Oklahoma State Fair (Fort Smith), Water Festival (Greers Ferry Lake), Ozark Frontier Trail Festival (Heber Springs), Riverfest (Little Rock), Arkansas State Fair and Livestock Show (Little Rock), Tontitown Grape Festival (Springdale).
Tours: Spring Tour of Historic Homes (Eureka Springs), Walking Tour (Hot Springs).
Theater: Arkansas Repertory Theatre (Little Rock), Ozark Mountain Music (Rogers).

Known as the *Hot Water State*, Arkansas is overflowing with rivers, lakes, and pure mountain springs. For years, Native Americans journeyed to the Hot Springs area to take advantage of the healing properties of the water; today, tourists visit to drink the water and to enjoy the thermal baths.

The Ozark Mountains, in northwestern Arkansas, have numerous springs, scenic plains, and rolling hills. Altitudes here can reach 2,000 feet.

The Land and the Climate

Arkansas is bordered on the north by Missouri, on the east by Tennessee and Mississippi, on the south by Louisiana, and on the west by Oklahoma and Texas. There are five main land regions in the state: the Ozark Plateau, the Ouachita Mountains, the Arkansas Valley, the Mississippi Alluvial Plain, and the West Gulf Coastal Plain.

The Ozark Plateau, also called the Ozark Mountains, is part of a large land region that Arkansas shares with Illinois, Missouri, and Oklahoma. In Arkansas the Plateau is a wide strip extending from the northwest through the north central part of the state. It is a beautiful region with its rugged hills, deep valleys, and rushing streams, much of it covered by dense hardwood and pine forests. This part of the state supports beef and dairy cattle, poultry farms, hay fields, and fruit orchards.

Arkansas

The Ouachita Mountains, in west-central Arkansas, extend into Oklahoma. This is a region of ridges and valleys, much of it unsuitable for farming. However, cattle, poultry, soybeans, and fruit can be raised where the land is not too steep. Timber is an important industry in the Ouachitas. Other resources here include sand, gravel, coal, and natural gas. This is also a region of hot springs and health resorts.

The Arkansas Valley lies between the Ozark Plateau and the Ouachita Mountains in the western two-thirds of the state. This hilly area includes the highest point in the state—Magazine Mountain, at 2,823 feet. The fertile fields here are ideal for raising vegetables, called truck crops, and there is good pasturage for beef cattle. Coal is mined in the Arkansas Valley, which also has extensive natural gas fields.

Arkansas' famous Hot Springs are in the Ouachita Mountains. At this well-known health and recreation resort, the waters reach a natural temperature of 143 degrees Fahrenheit.

The Mississippi Alluvial Plain stretches along the eastern border of Arkansas and is part of the Mississippi River delta that runs from Missouri through Louisiana. This is low, level, fertile land, ideal for growing cotton, rice, soybeans, oats, and wheat.

The West Gulf Coastal Plain covers southeast and south central Arkansas and extends into Louisiana and Texas. Here are pine forests, natural gas and oil deposits, and fruit, vegetable, livestock, and poultry farms.

The most important rivers in Arkansas are the Mississippi, which forms the state's eastern boundary, the Arkansas, the Ouachita, the Red, the White, and the St. Francis. Arkansas has a few large natural lakes and numerous man-made lakes. Many springs of pure water are found in the mountainous areas, including the state's famous Mammoth Springs and Hot Springs.

Crescent-shaped Lake Chicot, in southeastern Arkansas, is the state's largest natural body of water.

Temperatures in Arkansas vary considerably from north to south, although the entire state has a warm, rainy climate. In July temperatures range from 78 degrees Fahrenheit in the northwest to 82 degrees F. in the southern areas; January temperatures range between 36 degrees F. and 48 degrees F. Rainfall averages 48 inches per year, and little snow falls except in the highlands, which may receive some 6 inches per year.

The History

There were Paleo-Indians in what would become Arkansas several thousand years before Europeans explored the area in the 16th and 17th centuries. The Caddo and the Quapaw, or Arkansa, were the principal tribes encountered by the explorers.

The Spanish were the first non-Indians to arrive, in 1541. Hernando de Soto and his party discovered the Mississippi River after marching overland from Florida, and they crossed the river near what is now Memphis, Tennessee. De Soto went on through the Arkansas region to the Ozark Mountains. More than a century later, in 1673, the French explorers Father Jacques Marquette and Louis Joliet traveled down the Mississippi River to the Arkansas River. In 1682, Robert Cavelier, known as La Salle, claimed the lands along the Mississippi for France, calling the territory Louisiana. This claim included what would become Arkansas. In 1686 Henri de Tonti, a friend of La Salle, set up a camp that grew into the first non-Indian settlement west of the Mississippi, Arkansas Post, at the mouth of the Arkansas River.

Fort Smith was built in 1817 to protect settlers against Indian attacks. Seventy years later, natural gas was discovered in the area, which brought new prosperity to the state.

Jacques Marquette was one of the first Europeans to visit what is now Arkansas. In 1673 Marquette journeyed into the region briefly and glimpsed its beauties with his fellow explorer Louis Joliet.

The French made a few unsuccessful attempts at settlement after that, but in 1763 Spain took over the land west of the Mississippi. In 1800 the Louisiana Territory was returned to France, which sold it to the United States in 1803. When the U.S. government divided up the Louisiana Territory, what is now Arkansas became part of the Missouri Territory. Fort Smith was built in 1817 to protect Arkansas settlers from Indian attacks, and settlements began to rise between the fort and Arkansas Post. The Arkansas Territory, which included part of present-day Oklahoma, was created in 1819. In 1836 Arkansas became the 25th state of the Union, with Little Rock as its capital.

Arkansas was divided on the question of slavery: before the Civil War broke out in 1861, the state voted to remain in the Union.

Augustus H. Garland was governor of Arkansas from 1874 to 1876 and served as U.S. Attorney General during the 1880s. Throughout his career, Garland was a dedicated leader in the cause of civil and political rights.

Pioneer teacher Albert Pike established one of the first schools in Arkansas. Later, he became one of the state's best-known and most influential lawyers.

However, when the Union asked for troops, Arkansas refused to send them and seceded to join the Confederacy.

Even so, more than 10,000 Arkansas soldiers fought on the Union side during the war. Confederate troops in the state were forced into southern Arkansas after the Union victory at Pea Ridge in March 1862. Union troops captured Little Rock in 1863, and the Confederates set up a new capital at Washington, in southwestern Arkansas. The following year a Union state government was established at Little Rock by Arkansans opposed to the war, who drew up a new constitution that abolished slavery. These rival state governments continued until the war ended in 1865.

After the Civil War, federal troops occupied Arkansas from 1867 to 1874. During the late 1800s, the state's economy recovered from the years of conflict during and after the war and began to expand. Railroads were built, which brought new settlers into the state. Farming prospered, and the discovery of bauxite (aluminum ore) led to intensive mining. In the early 1900s, rice and soybean cultivation became important, as did the forest-products industry. Many former tenant farmers were able to buy land.

During World War II, farming and mining flourished to meet wartime demands, and new industries came into the state. By the 1950s the number of factories in Arkansas had doubled from the total operating before the United States entered the war in 1941. Arkansas was also an important area for training military personnel.

Today, Arkansas is still growing, economically and culturally. Petroleum, aluminum, processed foods, and forest products are integral parts of the state's economy. Tourism is increasingly important.

Education

The year after Arkansas became a territory, its first school, Dwight

Mission at Russellville, was established. The state legislature provided for a public-school system in 1843, the same year that the state's first library was founded in Little Rock.

The first schools for blacks were opened by the Freedmen's Bureau after 1864. In 1868, the state took control of these schools and founded a segregated, tax-supported school system. In 1954, the U.S. Supreme Court ruled that segregated public school systems are unconstitutional. In September 1954, federal troops forced the admission of nine black students to Central High School in Little Rock. In August 1958, a state law was passed permitting the closing of any school ordered to integrate student populations. All of the Little Rock high schools were closed during the 1958–59 school year. When they reopened in 1959 the schools began integrating students.

The first institution of higher education in Arkansas—Philander Smith College—was founded in 1868. By the turn of the century, there were six more colleges and universities in the state. In the 1980s Arkansas began to reform its public school system, one of the lowest ranked in the nation. School districts were consolidated and challenging standards were created. Unfortunately, the reluctance of the legislature to provide funds has impeded any significant progress.

General Douglas MacArthur, a native of Little Rock, became one of the nation's foremost military leaders. He commanded Allied forces in the Pacific theater of operations during World War II.

The People

Approximately 40 percent of Arkansans live in metropolitan areas. About 99 percent of them were born in the United States. The largest single religious group in the state is Baptist, followed by the Episcopalians, Methodists, Presbyterians, Roman Catholics, and members of the Churches of Christ.

Famous People

Many famous people were born in the state of Arkansas. Here are a few:

Lou Brock b. 1939, El Dorado. Hall of Fame baseball player

Helen Gurley Brown b. 1922, Green Forest. Magazine editor

Glen Campbell b. 1936, Billstown. Country singer

Johnny Cash b. 1932, Kingsland. Country singer

William Jefferson "Bill" Clinton b. 1946, Hope. First U.S. president from Arkansas

Dizzy Dean 1911-74, Lucas. Hall of Fame baseball pitcher

George E. Haynes 1880-1960, Pine Bluff. Civil rights leader

Alan Ladd 1913-64, Hot Springs. Film actor: *The Great Gatsby, Shane*

Laurence Luckinbill b. 1934, Fort Smith. Film actor: *The*

Boys in the Band, Such Good Friends

Douglas MacArthur 1880-1964, Little Rock. World War II and Korean War general

John McClellan 1896-1977, Sheridan. Senate leader

Dick Powell 1904-63, Mountain View. Film actor: *It Happened Tomorrow, Susan Slept Here*

Charlie Rich b. 1932, Forest City. Country singer

Brooks Robinson b. 1937, Little Rock. Hall of Fame baseball player

Sam Walton 1918-92, Little Rock. Founder of Wal-Mart stores

Colleges and Universities

There are many colleges and universities in Arkansas. Here are the more prominent, with their locations, dates of founding, and enrollments.

Arkansas State University, State University, 1909, 10,177

Arkansas Technical University, Russellville, 1909, 4,790

Harding University, Searcy, 1924, 3,463

Henderson State University, Arkadelphia, 1890, 3,434

John Brown University, Siloam Spring, 1919, 1,018

Southern Arkansas University, Magnolia, 1909, 2,742

University of Arkansas, Fayetteville, 1871, 14,582; *Little Rock,* 1927, 12,419; *Monticello,* 1909, 1,978; *Pine Bluff,* 1873, 3,709

University of Arkansas for Medical Sciences, Little Rock, 1879, 1,734

Where To Get More Information

Arkansas Chamber of Commerce
One Spring Building
Little Rock, AR 72201-2486
or call, 1-800-NATURAL

Kansas

The state seal of Kansas, adopted in 1861, is circular. In the center is a country scene in which the sun is rising over some hills. There is a river with a steamboat, a settler's cabin, an ox train and wagon, and a herd of buffalo being chased by two Indians. In the foreground is a man plowing the soil. The state motto appears over the picture, and around the circle is printed "Great Seal of the State of Kansas" and "January 29, 1861"—the date of Kansas' entry into the Union.

KANSAS
At a Glance

Capital: Topeka

Major Industries: Aircraft, petroleum products, farm machinery, agriculture

Major Crops: Wheat, sorghum, corn, hay

Size: 82,277 (14th largest)
Population: 2,522,574 (32nd largest)

State Flag

State Bird:
Western Meadowlark

State Flower:
Sunflower

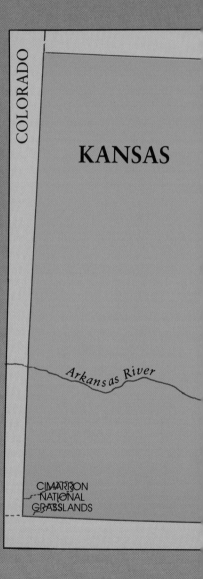

KANSAS

COLORADO

Arkansas River

CIMARRON
NATIONAL
GRASSLANDS

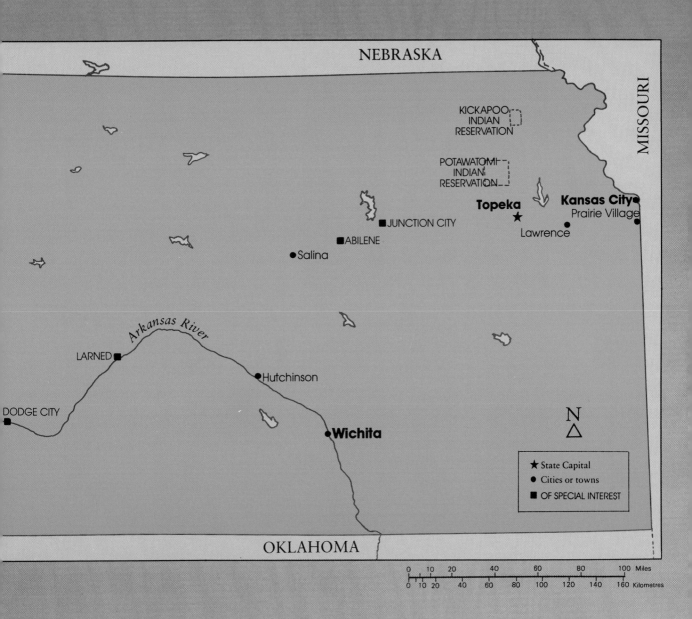

NEBRASKA

MISSOURI

KICKAPOO
INDIAN
RESERVATION

POTAWATOMI
INDIAN
RESERVATION

Topeka
★

■JUNCTION CITY

Kansas City●
Prairie Village

Lawrence●

■ABILENE

●Salina

Arkansas River

LARNED■

●Hutchinson

DODGE CITY
■

●Wichita

N
△

★ State Capital
● Cities or towns
■ OF SPECIAL INTEREST

OKLAHOMA

| 0 | 10 | 20 | | 40 | | 60 | | 80 | | 100 | Miles |
| 0 | 10 | 20 | 40 | 60 | 80 | 100 | 120 | 140 | 160 | Kilometres |

State Flag

The state flag, adopted in 1927 and amended in 1961, has the state seal in the center on a blue background. Below the seal is the word "Kansas," and above it is a sunflower.

State Banner

The state banner of Kansas, approved in 1925, is solid blue and has a sunflower in the center.

State Motto

Ad Astra per Aspera

This Latin motto can be translated as "To the stars through difficulties." It was adopted in 1861.

The green hills of Gypsum offer a contrast to the yellow prairie land that covers the central section of Kansas.

State Capital

Topeka has been the capital of Kansas since its entry into the Union in 1861.

State Name and Nicknames

The name Kansas comes from *Kanze*, which meant "south wind" in the Kansa Indian language.

Most commonly, Kansas is known as the *Sunflower State*, after the state flower. It has also been called *Bleeding Kansas* because of the fighting that occurred there before the Civil War. Other nicknames are the *Squatter State* (because of the squatters who settled there) and the *Jayhawker State* (after the pillagers who first occupied the territory).

State Flower

The sunflower, *Helianthus annuus*, was named the state flower of Kansas in 1903.

State Tree

The cottonwood, *Populus deltoides*, has been the state tree since 1937.

State Bird

School children voted the western meadowlark, *Sturnella neglecta*, to be the state bird, and it was adopted in 1937.

State Animal

In 1955, the American buffalo, *Bison americanus*, was selected as the state animal.

State Insect

Named in 1976, the honeybee, *Apis mellifera*, is the state insect.

State Song

"Home on the Range," with words by Dr. Brewster Higley and music by Dan Kelly, was adopted as state song in 1947.

State March

In 1935, Kansas designated "The Kansas March," by Duff E. Middleton, as state march.

Population

The population of Kansas in 1992 was 2,522,574, making it the 32nd most populous state.

There are 30.11 persons per square mile.

Industries

The principal industries of Kansas are agriculture, machinery, mining, and aerospace. The chief manufactured products are processed foods, aircraft, petroleum products, and farm machinery.

Agriculture

The chief crops of the state are wheat, sorghum, corn, and hay. Kansas is also a livestock state, and there are estimated to be some 5.65 million cattle, 1.44 million hogs and pigs, 179,000 sheep and lambs, and 1.8 million poultry on its farms. Oak and walnut trees are harvested. Cement, salt, and crushed stone are important mineral resources.

Government

The governor of Kansas is elected to a four-year term, as are the lieutenant governor, secretary of state, attorney general, treasurer, and commissioner of insurance. The state legislature, which meets annually, has a 40-member senate and a 125-member house of representatives. Senators serve four-year terms and representatives serve two-year terms. Each legislator is elected from a separate district. The most recent state constitution was adopted in 1859. In addition to its two U.S. senators, Kansas has four representatives in the U.S. House of Representatives. The state has six votes in the electoral college.

Sports

Kansas has long been a sports-minded state. The University of Kansas has won the NCAA championship in basketball (1952, 1988), and Wichita State University has won the NCAA baseball championship (1989).

Major Cities

Kansas City (population 149,800). Settled in 1843,

Kansas City is a manufacturing town, as evidenced by the presence of grain elevators, steel mills, automobile manufacturers, soap factories, railway yards, and other industries.

Things to see in Kansas City: Huron Indian Cemetery, Wyandotte County Historical Society and Museum, Agricultural Hall of Fame and National Center, Old Shawnee Town, and Community Nature Center Nature Trail.

Topeka (population 119,883). Founded in 1854, the capital city began as a terminus of the Atchison, Topeka and Santa Fe railroad. Today it is a manufacturing center and the home of the Menninger Foundation, the famous psychiatric clinic and research center.

Things to see in Topeka: State Capitol, Governor's Mansion, Kansas State Historical Society, Kansas Museum of History, Ward-Meade Historical Home, Gage Park, Topeka Zoo, and Potwin Place.

Wichita (population 304,017). Settled in 1868,

Wichita is best known for the manufacture of private aircraft. Originally, Wichita was an Indian trading post, and became a cow capital in the 1870s. Wichita is the most populous city in Kansas.

Things to see in Wichita: Century II, Wichita-Sedgwick County Historical Museum, Indian Center Museum, Omnisphere and Science Center, Wichita Art Museum, Wichita Art Association, Old Cowtown Museum, Sedgwick County Zoo and Botanical Garden, Clifton Square, Fellow-Reeve Museum of History and Science, Edwin A. Ulrich Museum of Art, and Lake Afton Public Observatory.

Places to Visit

The National Park Service maintains three areas in the state of Kansas: Fort Larned National Historic Site, Fort Scott National Historic Site, and Cimarron National Grasslands. In addition, there are 22 state recreation areas.

Abilene: Eisenhower Center. The Eisenhower family home contains original furnishings.

Atchison: International Forest of Friendship. A concrete path

Bell Hall is a college for military officers in Fort Leavenworth, the oldest permanent military post west of the Missouri River.

winds its way through the forest, which contains trees from 50 states and 33 countries.

Concordia: Brown Grand Opera House. This restored 1907 theater is in Renaissance style.

Council Grove: Pioneer Jail. Built in 1849, this was the only jail on the Santa Fe Trail.

Dodge City: Historic Front Street. This is a reconstruction of two blocks of the frontier town of the 1870s.

Hiawatha: Iowa, Sac and Fox Presbyterian Mission Museum. Built in 1837, this was one of the earliest Indian missions west of the Missouri River.

Independence: "Little House on the Prairie." This is a reproduction of Laura Ingalls Wilder's family home.

Leavenworth: Fort Leavenworth. The working fort also contains a museum of pioneer history and the Army of the West.

Liberal: Coronado Museum. This museum contains historical artifacts and Dorothy's house from *The Wizard of Oz.*

Marysville: Pony Express Barn Museum. Exhibits from the Pony Express days.

Medicine Lodge: Medicine Lodge Stockade. This is a replica of an 1874 stockade.

Norton: Station 15. This is a replica of an 1859 stagecoach depot.

Phillipsburg: Old Fort Bissell. Replicas of an Indian fort and sod house, a log cabin and schoolhouse.

Seneca: Fort Markley and Indian Village. This old western town contains a Victorian home, museum and art gallery.

Smith Center: Home on the Range Cabin. The restored cabin where Dr. Brewster Higley wrote the words for "Home on the Range."

Events

There are many events and organizations that schedule activities of various kinds in the state of Kansas. Here are some of them.

Sports: National Greyhound Meet (Abilene), Central Kansas Free Fair and PRCA Wild Bill Hickock Rodeo (Abilene), Inter-State Fair and Rodeo (Coffeyville), North Central Kansas Rodeo (Concordia), Rodeo (Hays), National Junior College Basketball Tournament (Hutchinson), Kansas Relays (Lawrence), International Pancake Race (Liberal), Riley County Fair and Kaw Valley Rodeo (Manhattan), McPherson County Fair and Rodeo

(McPherson), Virgil Herron Rodeo (Parsons), Rodeo (Phillipsburg), Tri-Rivers Fair and Rodeo (Salina), Huff 'n Puff Balloon Rally (Topeka), National Championship Baseball Tournament (Wichita).

Arts and Crafts: River Valley Art Festival (Arkansas City), Twin Rivers Festival (Emporia), Historic Preservation Association Antique Show and Flea Market (Fort Scott), Fine Arts Festival (Goodland), International Holiday Festival (Wichita).

Music: Bell Tower (Lawrence), Messiah Festival (Lindsborg),

The Kansas Cosmosphere & Discovery Center, in Hutchinson, is one of the state's most popular attractions.

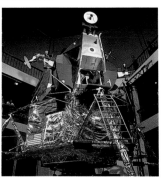

Bell Tower (Manhattan), Arts in the Park (Manhattan), Wichita Symphony Orchestra (Wichita), Jazz Festival (Wichita), Wichita River Festival (Wichita), Bluegrass Festival (Winfield).

Entertainment: Arkalalah Celebration (Arkansas City), Atchison County Fair (Atchison), Mexican Fiesta (Chanute), Fall Festival (Chanute), Dodge City Days (Dodge City), Long Branch Saloon (Dodge City), Good Ol' Days Celebration (Fort Scott), Pioneer Harvest Fiesta (Fort Scott), Beef Empire Days (Garden City), Mexican Fiesta (Garden City), Great Bend Frontier Festival (Great Bend), Halloween Parade (Hiawatha), Kansas State Fair (Hutchinson), Renaissance Festival (Kansas City), Buffalo Bill Cody Days (Leavenworth), Five-State Free Fair (Liberal), Mid-Summer's Day Festival (Lindsborg), St. Lucia Festival (Lindsborg), Indian Summer Days (Medicine Lodge), Bethel College Fall Festival (Newton), Mini-Sapa Days (Oberlin), John Brown Jamboree (Osawatomie), Smoky Hill River Festival (Salina), Steam Engine and Antique Farm Engine Show (Salina), Combat Air Museum Airshow and Superbatics (Topeka), Indian Powwow (Wichita), Octoberfest (Wichita), Christmas Through

Kansas is known for its sweeping fields of wheat, one of the state's most important crops.

the Windows at Old Cowtown Museum (Wichita), Cowley County Fair (Winfield).

Theater: Brown Grand Opera House (Concordia), Summer Theater (Emporia), Broadway R.F.D. (Lindsborg).

Though Kansas conjures up images of Dorothy's farm in *The Wizard of Oz,* the state has more than just gently rolling wheat farms and cattle ranches. The plains slope up into high hills and bluffs, recalling the more rugged image of the Old West.

The Land and the Climate

Kansas is bounded on the west by Colorado, on the north by Nebraska, on the east by Missouri, and on the south by Oklahoma. There are three main land regions in the state: the Dissected Till Plains, the Southeastern Plains, and the Great Plains.

The Dissected Till Plains are in the northeastern corner of Kansas, which was covered by great glaciers during the Ice Age. These glaciers left deposits of rich soil, rocks, and other material called till. Later, rivers cut through (dissected) the soil and left high bluffs. It is a region of farms that grow corn, hay, and sorghum. Hogs, dairy and beef cattle, and poultry are raised here.

The Southeastern Plains extend down from the Dissected Till Plains to the Oklahoma border. Here are gently sloping grass-covered hills—good grazing land for beef and dairy cattle. Sorghum and soybeans are grown in the region, which also has coal mines and natural gas wells.

The Great Plains cover the western two-thirds of Kansas. The land is slightly rolling, and slopes up from east to west, from about 1,500 feet above sea level to 4,000 feet at the Colorado border. This is wheat country; sorghum and sugar beets are also grown. Beef cattle and sheep are raised here, and there are oil and natural gas wells.

Kansas has two main river systems: the Kansas, or Kaw, and the Arkansas. Most of Kansas's 150 lakes are man-made.

Blizzards, thunderstorms, tornadoes, and hailstorms are not uncommon in Kansas, due to the rapid changes in temperature that can occur as a result of air masses sweeping across the plains. Winters are cold, with temperatures averaging 32 degrees Fahrenheit. July temperatures range from the high 70s to the low 90s. Snowfall averages 17 inches per year, with total precipitation varying between 18 inches in the west and 40 inches in the southeast.

Central Kansas combines high, hilly country and low-lying plains.

Much of western Kansas is vast, level prairie, ideal for grazing livestock. The state ranks among the nation's top four in total head of cattle.

The History

Kansas was named for the Kansa, or Kaw, Indians who once lived on its eastern plains, which were also inhabited by the Osage, Pawnee, and Wichita tribes. These Indians were buffalo hunters and farmers, who raised beans, corn, and squash. On the western plains were non-farming buffalo hunters who followed the great herds of bison, including the Arapaho, Cheyenne, Comanche, Kiowa, and other tribes.

Kansas was part of the vast area claimed by France in the late 1600s, after French explorers had ventured into the region, followed by French fur trappers in the early 1700s. Like the Spanish, the French did not establish permanent settlements.

Most of present-day Kansas was included when the United States bought the Louisiana Territory from France in 1803, although Spain claimed a small southwestern section. Peaceful farming and hunting Indians were still the territory's principal inhabitants. In 1835 the federal government took land from numerous tribes in the East and relocated them onto Kansas land, divided into reservations. The tribes native to Kansas were also crowded onto reservations, as part of the government's policy of Indian removal and appropriation of Indian land. By 1842 some 30 tribes had moved into the territory, including the Chippewa, Delaware, Fox, Iowa, Kickapoo, Ottawa, Potawatomi, Sauk, Shawnee, and Huron, or Wyandot. American missionaries and settlers soon flocked in by the Santa Fe Trail.

The first permanent non-Indian settlement was Fort Leavenworth, established in 1827. As homesteaders demanded still more land, the government moved the Indians west again, this time to Oklahoma, a long-time hunting ground of the Plains Indians. Both hardship and bloodshed ensued, as the Indians saw their land and way of life disappearing.

Nine sandstone buildings comprise Fort Larned, established in 1859. Many Kansas military posts were built to protect travellers on the Santa Fe Trail from Indian attacks.

Temperance crusader Carry Nation attracted national attention in the late 1800s by wrecking Kansas saloons with her hatchet.

In the elections of 1855, the pro-slavery group won control of the territorial legislature in Kansas with the help of illegal votes from citizens of Missouri, a slave state, who crossed the border to sway the election. In 1856 pro-slavery men burned part of the town of Lawrence, a Free State stronghold. The violent abolitionist John Brown raided Potawatomie Creek, and five pro-slavery men were killed. Similar clashes resulted in more than 50 deaths, as the entire country waited for news from "Bleeding Kansas."

Finally, the Free Staters gained control of the legislature and repealed the pro-slavery laws. But because the state was now predominantly Republican, Democrats in Congress did not admit Kansas as the 34th state until 1861, after several southern states had already left the Union.

During the Civil War, Confederate raiders under William C. Quantrill burned most of Lawrence and killed about 150 citizens. Kansas sent many soldiers to the Union Army—in proportion to its population, more than any other state.

After the war, Kansas opened land to Union veterans and to freed slaves. Railroads brought new settlers and access to Eastern markets. Longhorn cattle were driven to Kansas depots from their Texas pastures. A hardy strain of winter wheat called Turkey Red was introduced by Mennonite immigrants from Russia, and wheat farming flourished. Kansas towns like Abilene, Wichita, and Dodge City became symbols of the wild frontier. For 10 years after 1875, Dodge City was the largest cattle market in the world.

In the early 20th century, coal, zinc, and lead mining and drilling for oil and natural gas brought new income and industry to Kansas, but wheat farming remained the state's principal business. During the Great Depression of the 1930s, farm output declined, prices dropped, and many farmers had to declare bankruptcy. Banks failed and factories closed. A long drought caused a large area of the Kansas plains to become part of what was known as the Dust Bowl. But World War II brought demand for farm and mineral products from Kansas. War planes were produced in Wichita, and many military bases were built in the state.

Education

The first schools in the area currently known as Kansas were founded by Indians. In 1859 the state constitution provided for the establishment of elementary and secondary schools. There are six operating state universities, the most recent being Wichita State University founded in 1964. The University of Kansas in Lawrence is the largest. A foundation was laid in 1965 for the establishment of a statewide system of junior colleges. Today there are over 20 such schools. A number of private colleges exist in Kansas, but with the exception of the Washburn University of Topeka, most are church affiliated.

The People

Approximately 54 percent of Kansans live in metropolitan areas. Just over 97 percent of the residents were born in the United States. The largest religious groups are the Methodists and Roman Catholics, followed by the Baptists, Episcopalians, Lutherans, Presbyterians, and other Christian denominations.

Far left:
Aviator Amelia Earhart was a native of Atchison. She was the first woman to fly the Atlantic as a passenger and made aviation history as a pilot on long-distance solo flights.

Above:
Dwight D. Eisenhower, the 34th president of the United States, spent most of his childhood in Abilene, a major railroad center during the "cattle kingdom" days of the mid- to late 1800s.

Famous People

Many famous people were born in the state of Kansas. Here are a few:

Gwendolyn Brooks b. 1917, Topeka. Pulitzer Prize-winning poet: *Annie Allen, The Bean Eaters*

Walter P. Chrysler 1875-1940, Wamego. Automobile executive

Amelia Earhart 1897-1937, Atchison. Record-setting aviator

Dennis Hopper b. 1936, Dodge City. Film actor: *Easy Rider, Hoosiers*

William Inge 1913-73, Independence. Pulitzer Prize-winning novelist and playwright: *Picnic, The Dark at the Top of the Stairs*

Walter Johnson 1887-1946, Humboldt. Hall of Fame baseball pitcher

Buster Keaton 1896-1966, Piqua. Film actor: *The General, Limelight*

Emmett Kelly 1898-1979, Sedan. Circus clown

Charlie "Bird" Parker 1920-55, Kansas City. Jazz saxophonist

Damon Runyon 1880-1946, Manhattan. Short story writer: *Guys and Dolls, Money From Home*

Jim Ryun b. 1947, Wichita. Champion runner

Gayle Sayers b. 1943, Wichita. Hall of Fame football player

Earl W. Sutherland 1915-74, Burlingame. Nobel Prize-winning biochemist

John Cameron Swayze b. 1906, Wichita. Television newsman

Lyle Waggoner b. 1935, Kansas City. Television actor: *The Carol Burnett Show, Wonder Woman*

William Allen White 1868-1944, Emporia. Newspaper editor

Colleges and Universities

There are many colleges and universities in Kansas. Here are the more prominent, with their locations, dates of founding, and enrollments.

Emporia State University, Emporia, 1863, 6,006

Fort Hays State University, Hays, 1902, 5,603

Friends University, Wichita, 1898, 1,540

Kansas State University of Agriculture and Applied Science, Manhattan, 1863, 21,224

Pittsburg State University, Pittsburg, 1903, 6,515

Saint Mary College, Leavenworth, 1923, 1,023

University of Kansas, Lawrence, 1866, 29,161

Washburn University of Topeka, Topeka, 1865, 6,630

Wichita State University, Wichita, 1895, 15,120

Where To Get More Information

The Travel and Tourism Division, Department of Commerce & Housing 700 SW 8th St., Suite 1300 Topeka, KS 66603-3957 or call, 1-800-2KANSAS

Louisiana

The state seal of Louisiana, adopted in 1902, is circular. In the center is a picture of a female pelican protecting her three offspring. Above the pelican is "Union and Justice," and beneath is "Confidence." Around the edge of the seal is "State of Louisiana."

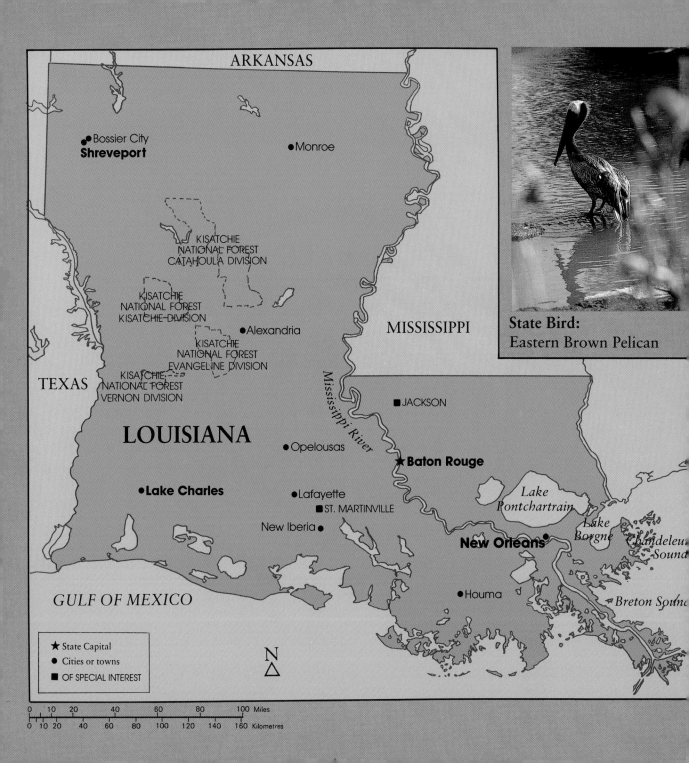

ARKANSAS

●Bossier City
Shreveport

●Monroe

KISATCHIE
NATIONAL FOREST
CATAHOULA DIVISION

KISATCHIE
NATIONAL FOREST
KISATCHIE DIVISION

●Alexandria

MISSISSIPPI

KISATCHIE
NATIONAL FOREST
EVANGELINE DIVISION

TEXAS

KISATCHIE
NATIONAL FOREST
VERNON DIVISION

■JACKSON

LOUISIANA

●Opelousas

Mississippi River

★**Baton Rouge**

●**Lake Charles**

●Lafayette
■ST. MARTINVILLE

New Iberia●

*Lake
Pontchartrain*

*Lake
Borgne*

*Chandeleur
Sound*

New Orleans●

GULF OF MEXICO

●Houma

Breton Sound

State Bird:
Eastern Brown Pelican

★ State Capital
● Cities or towns
■ OF SPECIAL INTEREST

N
△

0 10 20   40   60   80   100 Miles
0 10 20   40   60   80   100 120 140 160 Kilometres

LOUISIANA
At a Glance

State Flower: Magnolia

State Flag

Capital: Baton Rouge

Major Industries: Chemical products, transportation equipment, electronics, petroleum

Major Crops: Soybeans, sugarcane, rice, cotton

Size: 47,752 square miles (31st largest)
Population: 4,287,195 (21st largest)

41

State Flag

The state flag, adopted in 1912, bears the drawing from the state seal on a blue background. Beneath it is a white banner with the state motto.

State Motto

Union, Justice and Confidence
The motto was adopted in 1864. Previously, the motto had been *Justice, Union and Confidence*.

The day comes to a close in Louisiana, where the sunset stretches over bayou country.

State Capital
 The first capital of
Louisiana was New Orleans
(1812-30). Then came
Donaldsonville (1830-31),
New Orleans again (1831-49),
Baton Rouge (1849-62), and
New Orleans yet again
(1862-82). Finally, Baton
Rouge became the capital
again, and has remained so
ever since.

State Name and Nicknames
 Robert Cavelier, Sieur de la
Salle, claimed the Mississippi
Valley for France in 1682,
naming it La Louisianne for
King Louis XIV of France.
 Louisiana has several
nicknames, but the most
common one is the *Pelican
State*, after the state bird. *Bayou
State* refers to the number of
bayous, and the *Fisherman's
Paradise* refers to the excellent
fishing waters in the state. It
has also been called the *Child of
the Mississippi* because of its
geological origin, and the
Sugar State because of the
importance of that crop.

State Flower
 The magnolia, *Magnolia
grandiflora*, was named the
state flower in 1900.

State Tree
 The bald cypress, *Taxodium
distichum*, was adopted as the
state tree in 1963.

State Bird
 The eastern brown pelican,
Pelecanus occidentalis, became
the state bird in 1966.
Previously, the pelican, with
no specific type mentioned,
had been the state bird.

State Crustacean
 The crawfish (or crayfish—
family *Astacidae*) has been
the state crustacean since
1983.

State Dog
 In 1979, the Louisiana
Catahoula leopard dog was
adopted as state dog.

State Drink
 Milk was made the state
drink in 1983.

State Fossil
 In 1976, petrified palmwood
was adopted as state fossil.

State Gem
 The agate has been the state
gem since 1976.

State Insect
 The honeybee, *Apis mellifera*,
became the state insect in
1977.

State Songs
 Louisiana has two state
songs, "Give Me Louisiana,"
by Doralice Fontane, and
"You Are My Sunshine," by
Jimmie H. Davis and Charles
Mitchell.

Population
 The population of Louisiana
in 1992 was 4,287,195, making
it the 21st most populous
state. There are 81.4 persons
per square mile. About 69
percent of Louisianans live in
metropolitan areas. Culturally,
Louisiana can be considered
two states: a French, Roman
Catholic south and an Anglo-
Saxon, Protestant north.

Another southern group is descended from the French settlers who were driven from the Acadian section of Canada by the British in 1755—the Cajuns. Many Louisianans speak both French and English.

Industries

The principal industries of Louisiana are trade, construction, transportation, and mining. The chief manufactured products are chemical products, foods, transportation equipment, electronic equipment, apparel, and petroleum products.

Agriculture

The chief crops of the state are soybean, sugarcane, rice, corn, cotton, sweet potatoes, melons, and pecans. Louisiana is also a livestock state, and there are estimated to be some 1.02 million cattle, 60,000 hogs and pigs, 16,000 sheep, and 1.85 million poultry on its farms. Pine, hardwood, and oak trees are harvested.

Salt, sand, gravel, and sulphur are important mineral resources. Commercial fishing earned $295 million in 1992.

Government

The governor of Louisiana is elected to a four-year term, as are the lieutenant governor, secretary of state, attorney general, treasurer, commissioner of agriculture, and superintendent of education. The state legislature, which meets annually, consists of a 39-member senate and a 105-member house of representatives. Senators and representatives serve four-year terms, and are elected from 39 senatorial districts and 105 representative districts. The most recent state constitution was adopted in 1974 and has one of the most liberal Bill of Rights in the nation. Louisiana has had 11 constitutions—more than any other state—many of which were drawn to create

specific laws. In addition Louisiana has seven representatives in the House of Representatives. The state has nine votes in the electoral college.

Sports

Louisiana is a sports state, especially in football. Every year the Sugar Bowl is held in New Orleans. It has been won by Tulane (1935) and Louisiana State University (1959, 1965, 1968). In addition, LSU has won the Cotton Bowl (1963, 1966) and Orange Bowl (1944, 1962).

On the professional level, the New Orleans Saints of the National Football League play in the Superdome.

Major Cities

Baton Rouge (population 219,531). Founded in 1719, the capital city was settled by the French. Today it is a major Mississippi River port and an industrial center. The city has beautiful antebellum mansions and gardens.
Things to see in Baton Rouge: Oakley (1799), State Capitol,

Governor's Mansion, Louisiana Arts and Science Center, Old Governor's Mansion, Laurens Henry Cohn Sr. Memorial Plant Arboretum, Greater Baton Rouge Zoo, Magnolia Mound Plantation, Mount Hope Plantation, Rural Life Museum, USS *Kidd*, Heritage Museum and Village, Parlange Plantation (1750), Nottoway Plantation (1859), and Glynnwood Plantation Home.

New Orleans (population 496,938). Founded in 1718 by Jean Baptiste le Moyne, the city was named LaNouvelle Orleans in honor of Philippe, Duke d'Orleans. The state's largest city, it was settled by French and Spanish who called themselves Creole to indicate that they were of unmixed French or Spanish ancestry. This cosmopolitan city with an old-world charm in its French Quarter attracts millions of tourists for Mardi Gras, two weeks of festivities that precede the Christian period of Lent. In addition to being a tourist attraction, New Orleans is one of the busiest ports in the United States and it prospers as a NASA space-flight center.

Things to see in New Orleans: Jackson Square, Jackson Brewery, Cabildo (1795), Pirate's Alley, St. Louis Cathedral (1794), Presbytère (1791), French Market, Old U.S. Mint, Madame John's Legacy (1727), Adelina Patti's House and Courtyard, Court of Two Sisters, Historic New Orleans Collection, Old Absinthe House, Louis Armstrong Park, Preservation Hall, Levee and docks, Barataria Unit, New Orleans Museum of Art, Dueling Oaks, Garden District, Audubon Park and Zoological Gardens, World Trade Center of New Orleans, Pharmacy Museum (1823), Confederate Museum, and St. Charles Avenue Streetcar.

Shreveport (population 198,525). Founded in 1839, Shreveport was originally a thriving river town. Now it is an industrial center and a lumber-producing center.

Things to see in Shreveport: Louisiana State Exhibit Museum, Veteran's Park, C. Bickham Dickson Park, R. S. Barnwell Memorial Garden and Art Center, R. W. Norton Art Gallery, American Rose Center, and Water Town.

Places to Visit

The National Park Service maintains two areas in the state of Louisiana: Jean Lafitte National Historical Park and Preserve, and Kisatchie National Forest. In addition, there are 14 state recreation areas.

Alexandria: Kent House. Built in 1800, this is a restored French Colonial plantation.

Franklin: Arlington Plantation. This Greek Revival mansion, built in 1840, stands on the banks of the Bayou Teche.

Jackson: Asphodel Plantation. Built from 1820 to 1830, this antebellum mansion accepts overnight guests.

Lafayette: Acadian Village: A Museum of Acadian Heritage and Culture. This restored bayou town contains houses, a general store, and a chapel.

Lake Charles: "Charpentier" Historical District. Victorian homes are located in 40 square blocks of downtown.

Many: Hodges Gardens. Wild and cultivated flowers cover 4,700 acres.

Minden: Germantown Museum. Three buildings, built in 1835

Louisiana

The French Quarter, with the elaborate ironwork on its buildings and exciting nightlife on its streets, is the cultural center of New Orleans.

by German settlers, contain records and artifacts of the original inhabitants.

Morgan City: Swamp Gardens and Wildlife Zoo. This outdoor swamp museum depicts the history of the Atchafalaya Basin.

Natchitoches: Fort St. Jean Baptiste State Commemorative Area. This replica of the 1732 fort includes a barracks, chapel, and Indian huts.

New Iberia: Shadows-on-the-Teche. Built in 1834, this is a Classical Revival home.

Opelousas: Jim Bowie Museum. This museum contains Bowie memorabilia.

Events

There are many events and organizations that schedule activities of various kinds in the state of Louisiana. Here are some of them.

Sports: Super Derby Festival (Bossier City), Southwest Fat Stock Show and Rodeo (Lake Charles), Contraband Days (Lake Charles), Sugar Bowl College Football Classic (New Orleans).

Arts and Crafts: FestForAll (Baton Rouge), Fall Crafts Festival (Baton Rouge), Lagniappe on the Bayou (Houma), Azalea Trail (Lafayette), Red River Revel Arts Festival (Shreveport).

Music: River City Blues Festival (Baton Rouge), Cajun Country Outdoor Opry and Fais Do Do (Houma), New Orleans Opera Association (New Orleans), New Orleans Symphony (New Orleans), New Orleans Jazz and Heritage Festival (New Orleans).

Entertainment: North Louisiana Cotton Festival and Fair (Bastrop), International Acadian Festival (Baton Rouge), Greater Baton Rouge State Fair (Baton Rouge), Taste of the Bayou (Houma), Blessing of the Shrimp Fleet (Houma), International Rice Festival (Lafayette), Battle of Pleasant Hill Reenactment (Many), Sawmill Days (Many), Sabine Free State Festival (Many), Louisiana Shrimp and Petroleum Festival and Fair (Morgan City), Natchitoches-Northwestern Folk Festival (Natchitoches), Christmas Festival of Lights (Natchitoches), Sugarcane Festival and Fair (New Iberia), Mardi Gras (New Orleans), French Quarter Festival (New Orleans), Spring Fiesta (New Orleans), Louisiana Yambilee (Opelousas), Louisiana Peach Festival (Ruston), Festa Italiana (Shreveport), Louisiana State Fair (Shreveport), Christmas in Roseland (Shreveport).

Tours: Annie Miller's Swamp and Marsh Tours (Houma), Natchitoches Pilgrimage (Natchitoches), Historic Washington Annual Pilgrimage (Opelousas), Audubon Pilgrimage (St. Francisville).

Theater: Louisiana Passion Play (Calhoun), Festival International de Louisiane (Lafayette), Le Petit Theatre du Vieux Carré (New Orleans), Saenger Performing Arts Center (New Orleans).

The state with the third-longest tidal shoreline, Louisiana abounds with rivers, marshes, lakes, bays, and bayous—not surprisingly, then, the state has been nicknamed the *Pelican State,* the *Bayou State,* the *Child of the Mississippi,* and the *Fisherman's Paradise.*

The Land and the Climate

Louisiana's marshy coastal region, in the southern part of the state, is dotted with lagoons and lakes.

Slow-moving bodies of water called *bayous* help drain Louisiana's many swamps.

Louisiana is bordered on the west by Texas, on the north by Arkansas, on the east by Mississippi, and on the south by the Gulf of Mexico. The state has three main land regions: the East Gulf Coastal Plain, the Mississippi Alluvial Plain, and the West Gulf Coastal Plain.

The East Gulf Coastal Plain is located east of the Mississippi River and north of Lake Pontchartrain. Its southern section has extensive marshland, rising to low hills in the north.

The Mississippi Alluvial Plain is located along the lower Mississippi River, extending north and south from the Arkansas line to the Gulf of Mexico. The region contains broad, low ridges and hollows and, to the south, the great Mississippi Delta—formed by silt carried down to the mouth of the river. Here is some of the most fertile soil in Louisiana.

The West Gulf Coastal Plain comprises the western half of the state. In the south it is a region of marshes. Farther north are the Louisiana prairies, succeeded by higher land extending toward Arkansas. A variety of farms in western Louisiana produce grain crops, peanuts, and beef and dairy cattle. Industry benefits from oil and natural gas wells and extensive stands of timber.

Louisiana's coastline measures some 397 miles in length. But if the bays, offshore islands, and river mouths are included, the coastline is 7,721 miles long. Only Alaska and Florida have longer tidal shorelines. The most important rivers in the state are the Mississippi, the Atchafalaya, and the Red. The largest lake in the state is Lake Pontchartrain, once an arm of the sea, which is filled with salt water. Numerous bayous in the Mississippi Delta drain excess water from the region's lakes and rivers. Louisiana, with 53 inches of rainfall annually, is one of the wettest states in the country. Hot and humid in the summer, southern Louisiana has temperatures of more than 80 degrees Fahrenheit. Winter temperatures rarely fall below 50 to 55 degrees F.

The History

When the first European explorers arrived, some 12,000 Indians were living in what was to become Louisiana. They belonged to several dozen tribes, among them the Atakapa, the Caddo, the Chitimacha, and the Tunica. Most of them lived on the banks of rivers and bayous, where they built huts of poles and palmetto leaves, sometimes plastered with mud. To provide food, the women farmed, and the men hunted and fished.

The Spanish explorer Hernando de Soto was the first European to see the Louisiana area, when he arrived in 1541 on a fruitless search for gold. He died there the next year, and the Spanish made no attempt to explore the territory further. The French explorer Robert Cavelier, called La Salle, arrived in 1682 with his band of 50 men. They had come down the Mississippi from the Great Lakes region. La Salle claimed the vast Mississippi Valley for France, naming it Louisiana for King Louis XIV.

Pierre Le Moyne, known as d'Iberville, came to the region in 1699, founding a French settlement at what is now Ocean Springs, Mississippi. The first permanent non-Indian settlement in present-day Louisiana was made by French colonists on the Red River at Natchitoches in 1714. In 1718 the governor of Louisiana, d'Iberville's brother, Jean Baptiste Le Moyne, began to construct New Orleans at the mouth of the Mississippi River. The new city became the capital of the colony in 1722.

France was disappointed in the financial return on its investment in the colony, and in 1762 it ceded to Spain the Isle of Orleans, which included New Orleans, and Louisiana land west of the Mississippi River. Under Spanish rule, Louisiana prospered and developed an important sugar industry. But in 1800 France renewed its interest in the region and negotiated with Spain to return the territory, which it did in 1803. France then promptly sold the entire Louisiana Territory to the United States for about $15 million. French and Spanish

Beginning in 1701, French Louisiana was governed by Jean Baptiste Le Moyne, who founded New Orleans in 1718. He named it in honor of the Duc d'Orleans, regent of France.

The Battle of New Orleans, on January 8, 1815, was a resounding victory over the British for American general Andrew Jackson and his forces in the last action of the War of 1812.

Huey Long, governor of Louisiana from 1928 to 1932 and U.S. senator from 1932 to 1935, was one of the state's most powerful political figures. Long, born in Winnifield, established a "political machine" that gave him almost total control of state government.

settlers were surprised to learn that their homeland was becoming part of the United States. By this time some 4,000 French residents of Acadia, eastern Canada—the Cajuns, as they were called—had moved into Louisiana.

In 1804 Congress divided up the Louisiana Territory, and one part became the Territory of Orleans, which was about the same area as the present state of Louisiana. In 1812 the territory was admitted to the Union as the 18th state. During the War of 1812, the British tried to capture the port of New Orleans in a battle that began in December 1814. On January 8, 1815, the British were defeated by General Andrew Jackson and his 4500-man force of frontiersmen. Neither side was aware that the victory occurred two weeks after a peace treaty had been signed by the United States and Great Britain.

The Civil War, in which Louisiana left the Union to join the Confederacy in 1861, ruined the state's economy, which had prospered as a result of heavy steamboat traffic on the Mississippi beginning in 1812. Union forces occupied New Orleans in 1862 and eventually controlled the entire state. There was widespread destruction of property. Not until the late 19th century did the economy begin to recover, as railroads expanded, roads and waterways were improved, and commerce resumed. Oil was discovered in 1901, and natural gas in 1916.

During World War II, many new industries began, including shipbuilding. The chemical and oil industries boomed. In the years between 1940 and 1960, the number of factories and plants increased about 60 percent. Today, Louisiana is still prospering as a center of national and international commerce. The addition of new products, as in the aerospace industry, has contributed to its growth.

Education

The first school in what is now Louisiana was founded in New Orleans in 1725 by Roman Catholic monks. In 1727 Ursuline nuns

Perhaps the best-known feature of Louisiana's social life is the week-long succession of parades and festivals called Mardi Gras. Held each year before Lent, the New Orleans carnival attracts thousands of visitors to the city.

started a girls' school that is still operating. The first public school was established by the Spanish in 1772, and in 1845 the statewide public school system began. Louisiana's first library opened in New Orleans in 1804, and the New Orleans Public Library, established in 1843, was the state's first free library.

Famous People

Many famous people were born in the state of Louisiana. Here are a few:

Louis "Satchmo" Armstrong 1900-71, New Orleans. Jazz trumpeter

Terry Bradshaw spent his career as quarterback for the Pittsburgh Steelers.

Pierre G. T. Beauregard 1818-93, near New Orleans. Confederate general

Terry Bradshaw b. 1948, Shreveport. Hall of Fame football player

Truman Capote 1924-84, New Orleans. Author: *In Cold Blood, Breakfast at Tiffany's*

Van Cliburn b. 1934, Shreveport. Concert pianist

Michael DeBakey b. 1908, Lake Charles. Heart transplant surgeon

Fats Domino b. 1928, New Orleans. Singer

Louis Moreau Gottschalk 1829-69, New Orleans.

Pianist and composer

Bryant Gumbel b. 1948, New Orleans. Television host

Elvin Hayes b. 1945, Rayville.

Playwright Lillian Hellman, born in New Orleans, wrote such powerful dramas as *The Little Foxes* (1939) and *Watch on the Rhine* (1941).

Hall of Fame basketball player

Lillian Hellman 1905-84, New Orleans. Dramatist: *Watch on the Rhine, The Little Foxes*

Al Hirt b. 1922, New Orleans. Jazz trumpeter

Mahalia Jackson 1911-72, New Orleans. Gospel singer

Dorothy Lamour b. 1914, New Orleans. Film actress: *The Hurricane, Road to Singapore*

Huddie "Leadbelly" Ledbetter 1888?-1949, near Shreveport. Folk singer and composer

Jerry Lee Lewis b. 1935, Ferriday. Rock singer

Huey Long 1893-1935, Winnfield. Public official

King Oliver 1885-1938, near New Orleans. Jazz cornetist

Mel Ott 1909-58, Gretna. Hall of Fame baseball player

Willis Reed b. 1942, Hico.

Hall of Fame basketball player

Bill Russell b. 1934, Monroe. Hall of Fame basketball player

Edward D. White 1845-1921, Lafourche Parish. Chief Justice of the Supreme Court

Andrew Young b. 1932, New Orleans. Ambassador to the United Nations

Colleges and Universities

There are many colleges and universities in Louisiana. Here are the more prominent, with their locations, dates of founding, and enrollments.

Centenary College of Louisiana, Shreveport, 1825, 1,048

Louisiana State University and A&M College, Baton Rouge, 1860, 26,607

Louisiana State University in Shreveport, 1965, 4,665

Louisiana Technical University, Ruston, 1894, 10,263

Loyola University, New

Orleans, 1912, 5,582

McNeese State University, Lake Charles, 1939, 8,474

Northeast Louisiana University, Monroe, 1931, 11,732

Northwestern State University of Louisiana, Natchitoches, 1884, 8,412

Southeastern Louisiana University, Hammond, 1925, 12,847

Southern University and A&M College, Baton Rouge, 1880, 10,000

Tulane University of Louisiana, New Orleans, 1834, 11,345

University of Southwestern Louisiana, Lafayette, 1898, 15,677

Xavier University of Louisiana, New Orleans, 1925, 3,330

Where To Get More Information

Department of Culture, Recreation and Tourism Louisiana Office of Tourism P.O. Box 94291 Baton Rouge, LA 70804-9291 Or Call 1-800-33-GUMBO

Missouri

The state seal of Missouri dates back to 1822. It is circular. In the center is a small circle with a bear and crescent on the left and the arms of the United States on the right. Around the circle is printed "United We Stand, Divided We Fall." The circle is flanked on each side by a grizzly bear. Underneath is a banner with the state motto and the date "MDCCCXX" (1820—the year of the first constitution). Atop the circle is a helmet, and above that are 24 stars, showing that Missouri was the 24th state in the Union. Around the seal is printed "Great Seal of the State of Missouri."

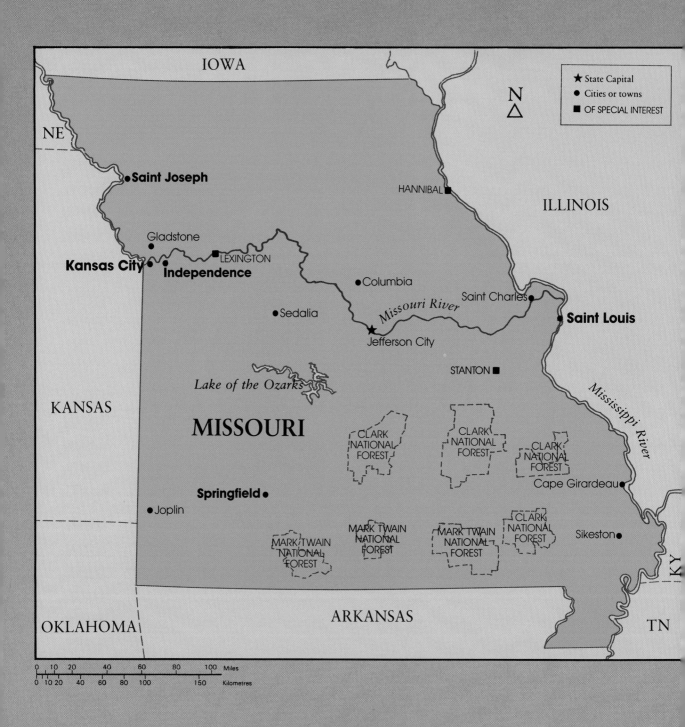

IOWA

NE

Saint Joseph

HANNIBAL ■

ILLINOIS

Gladstone

■ LEXINGTON

Kansas City

Independence

Columbia

Saint Charles

Missouri River

Sedalia

Saint Louis

★ Jefferson City

Mississippi River

STANTON ■

KANSAS

Lake of the Ozarks

MISSOURI

CLARK
NATIONAL
FOREST

CLARK
NATIONAL
FOREST

CLARK
NATIONAL
FOREST

Cape Girardeau

Springfield ●

Joplin

Sikeston ●

MARK TWAIN
NATIONAL
FOREST

MARK TWAIN
NATIONAL
FOREST

MARK TWAIN
NATIONAL
FOREST

CLARK
NATIONAL
FOREST

KY

OKLAHOMA

ARKANSAS

TN

N
△

★ State Capital
● Cities or towns
■ OF SPECIAL INTEREST

| 0 | 10 | 20 | 40 | 60 | 80 | 100 | Miles |
| 0 | 10 | 20 | 40 | 60 | 80 | 100 | 150 | Kilometres |

MISSOURI
At a Glance

State Flag

State Flower: Hawthorn

Capital: Jefferson City

Major Industries: Transportation equipment, electronics, chemicals, agriculture

Major Crops: Soybeans, corn, wheat, cotton

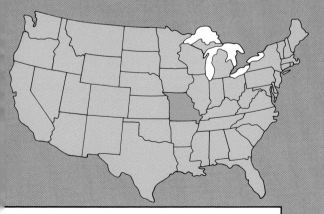

State Bird: Bluebird

Size: 69,697 square miles (19th largest)
Population: 5,192,632 (15th largest)

57

State Flag
The state flag, adopted in 1913, has three horizontal stripes: red, white, and blue. In the center is the state seal surrounded by a blue ring containing 24 white stars.

State Motto
Salus Populi Suprema Lex Esto
This Latin motto, adopted in 1822, means "The welfare of the people shall be the supreme Law."

Big Spring is a scenic area near Van Buren.

State Capital

St. Charles was the capital of Missouri from 1821 (when it became a state) until 1826, when Jefferson City was selected.

State Name and Nicknames

The state was named for the Missouri River, which, in turn, was named for the Missouri Indians.

The most common nickname for Missouri is the *Show Me State*, which denotes stubbornness accompanied by common sense.

Other nicknames include *Center State*; *Gateway to the West*; and *Mother of the West*.

State Flower

Adopted in 1923, the state flower is the red haw, wild haw, or hawthorn blossom, *Crataegus*.

State Tree

The flowering dogwood, *Cornus florida*, was named the state tree in 1955.

State Bird

The bluebird, *Sialia sialis*, has been the state bird since 1927.

State Mineral

In 1967, galena, an ore of lead, was selected as the state mineral.

State Rock

Mozarkite was named the state rock in 1967.

State Fossil

The crinoid, or sea lily, was designated state fossil in 1989. It is related to the starfish.

State Insect

The honeybee, *Apis mellifera*, was selected as the official state insect in 1985.

State Musical Instrument

In 1987, the fiddle was chosen state musical instrument.

State Tree Nut

The Eastern Black Walnut, *juglans nigra*, was chosen official tree nut of Missouri in 1990.

State Song

"Missouri Waltz," with music by John Valentine Eppel and words by J. R. Shannon, was adopted as state song in 1949.

Population

The population of Missouri in 1992 was 5,192,632, making it the 15th most populous state. There are 73.41 persons per square mile.

Industries

The principal industries of the state of Missouri are agriculture, tourism, and aerospace. The chief manufactured products are transportation equipment, food products, electrical and electronic equipment, and chemicals.

Agriculture

The chief crops of the state are soybeans, corn, wheat, and cotton. Missouri is also a livestock state, and there are estimated to be some 4.5 million cattle, 2.7 million hogs and pigs, 111,000 sheep, 7.6 million chickens and eggs, and 21.5 million turkeys

on its farms.
Oak and hickory trees are harvested. Crushed stone, limestone, lead, zinc, and copper are important mineral resources.

Government

The governor of Missouri is elected to a four-year term, as are the lieutenant governor, secretary of state, state treasurer, attorney general, and state auditor. The state legislature, or general assembly, which meets annually, consists of a senate of 34 members and a house of representatives of 163 members. Senators, who serve four-year terms, are elected from 34 senatorial districts, and representatives, who serve two-year terms, are elected from 163 representative districts. The most recent state constitution was adopted in 1945. In addition to its two U.S. senators, Missouri has nine representatives in the U.S. House of Representatives. The state has 11 votes in the electoral college.

Sports

Missouri has always been a sports-minded state. On the professional level, the St. Louis Cardinals of the National League play baseball in Busch Stadium and the Kansas City Royals of the American League play in Royals Stadium. In football, the Kansas City Chiefs of the National Football League play in Arrowhead Stadium. The St. Louis Blues of the National Hockey League play in the St. Louis Arena.

Major Cities

Independence (population 112,301). Chosen as the seat of Jackson County in 1827, Independence was incorporated in 1849. In the 1830s it became a staging area for wagon trains headed for the Pacific Coast. In 1846 it was linked to Santa Fe by an overland mail stagecoach line. Today it is a residential and manufacturing community.

Things to see in Independence: Old log courthouse and the home of former president Harry S. Truman

Jefferson City (population 35,517). Settled around 1823, it was originally a small river settlement named for Thomas Jefferson. It was selected as the state capital in 1821, when it contained only a foundry, shop, and mission. Today, "Jeff City" is a prosperous small town whose chief activity is government.

Things to see in Jefferson City: Governors mansion, Cole County Historical Society Museum, State Capitol, Missouri State Museum, Missouri Veterinary Medical Foundation Museum.

Saint Joseph is the home of the Stetson Hat Company.

Kansas City (population 434,829). Settled in 1838, Kansas City was once a trading post. Originally occupied by the Kansa Indians, its initial population growth was due to westward expansion and the gold-hungry "49ers," and it became a boom town when the railroads arrived. Its economy was diversified by many kinds of manufacturing activities in the 20th century. It is second only to Detroit in automobile assembly. It is a center of foreign trade due to tariff advantages and houses extensive assembly warehousing facilities. Today it is a city with broad streets and beautiful parks.

Things to see in Kansas City:
Kansas City Museum, Liberty Memorial Museum, Toy and Miniature Museum, Nelson-Atkins Museum of Art, Antiques and Art Center, Kansas City Art Institute (1885), City Market, Kaleidoscope, Union Cemetery (1857), Kansas City Zoo, Benjamin Ranch, Van Ackeren Gallery, and Jesse James Bank Museum.

St. Louis (population 396,685). Settled in 1764, St. Louis was originally a fur-trading post. Founded by Pierre Laclede, a merchant from New Orleans, he explored the Mississippi River in search of a trading post for his company. The site was named in honor of King Louis XV of France. In 1804, it was the site of the official transfer of Louisiana to the United States, and 100 years later it was the scene of the St. Louis World's Fair—the Louisiana Purchase Exposition.

The most populous Missouri city, its economy has been fairly stable during economically troubled times, though it has lagged behind other metropolitan areas since Word War II. Today it is a transportation, manufacturing, retail, and educational center. St. Louis is the site of the country's busiest inland port.

Things to see in St. Louis:
St. Louis Science Center, Missouri Historical Society, St. Louis Art Museum, St. Louis Zoological Park,

Gateway Arch, Museum of Westward Expansion, Eads Bridge (1874), Riverboat *President*, Americana Emporium, Eugene Field House and Toy Museum (1845), St. Louis Sports Hall of Fame, National Bowling Hall of Fame, St. Louis Union Station, Missouri Botanical Garden, Jefferson Barracks Historical Park, Mercantile Money Museum, Purina Farms, Dog Museum, and Mastodon State Park.

The Mark Twain Home and Museum, located in Hannibal, is the boyhood home of this great American writer, and it contains many mementoes of his life and travels.

Places to Visit

The National Park Service maintains six areas in the state of Missouri: Jefferson National Expansion Memorial, Ozark National Scenic Riverways, Wilson's Creek National Battlefield, George Washington Carver National Monument, Harry S. Truman National Historic Site, and Mark Twain National Forest. In addition, there are 40 state recreation areas.

Hannibal: Mark Twain Museum and Boyhood Home. The great writer lived here in the 1840s and 1850s.

Independence: The Harry S. Truman Library and Museum. One of the exhibits is a reproduction of Truman's White House office.

Lamar: Harry S. Truman Birthplace State Historic Site.

Lexington: Lafayette County Courthouse. Built in 1847, this is the oldest courthouse in constant use west of the Mississippi.

Monroe City: Mark Twain Birthplace and State Park. The park grounds include the two-room house where the author was born.

Osage Beach: Indian Burial Cave. A boat ride through an archeological cave.

St. Joseph: Jesse James Home. The cottage where the outlaw lived and was shot to death.

Sullivan: Meramec Caverns. These caverns were used as a Civil War gunpowder plant and a hideout by Jesse James in the 1870s.

Events

There are many events and organizations that schedule activities in the state of Missouri. Here are some of them.

Sports: American Royal Livestock, Horse Show, and Rodeo (Kansas City), Bootheel Rodeo (Sikeston).

Arts and Crafts: National Crafts Festival (Branson), Rose Week (Cape Girardeau), Columbia Art League Art Fair (Columbia), Prairie View Festival (St. Joseph), Watercolor USA (Springfield).

Music: Baldknobbers Hillbilly Jamboree (Branson), Lyric Opera (Kansas City), Kansas City Symphony (Kansas City), Kansas City Jazz Festival (Kansas City), State Ballet of Missouri (Kansas City), Opera Theatre of St. Louis (St. Louis), St. Louis Symphony (St. Louis), National Classic Jazz and Ragtime Festival (St. Louis), Muny Opera (St. Louis), Springfield Symphony (Springfield).

Entertainment: Riverfest (Cape Girardeau), Tom Sawyer Days (Hannibal), Truman Week Celebration (Independence), Ethnic Enrichment Festival (Kansas City), Battle of Lexington Reenactment (Lexington), Joseph Robidoux Festival (St. Joseph), Strassenfest (St. Louis), Hot Air Balloon Race (St. Louis), Missouri State Fair (Sedalia).

Tours: Walking Tour (Arrow Rock), Jour de Fête à Ste. Geneviève (Sainte Genevieve).

Theater: Old Mill Theater (Branson), Mark Twain Outdoor Theater (Hannibal), Molly Brown Dinner Theater (Hannibal), Missouri Repertory Theatre (Kansas City), Coterie Children's Theater (Kansas City), Starlight Theater (Kansas City), Repertory Theatre of St. Louis (St. Louis), Theatre Project Company (St. Louis), Tent Theater (Springfield).

A quaint covered bridge reminiscent of another age. Missouri played a large role in the history of the Old West. Many of the state's cities originated as trading posts, founded by frontiersmen such as Daniel Boone, and served as departure points for wagon trains headed west.

The Lake of the Ozarks, in west-central Missouri, is the state's largest man-made lake. This region draws many vacationers to its attractive resorts.

Southeastern Missouri is part of the Mississippi Alluvial Plain and has the rich soil of a great river delta.

The Land and the Climate

Missouri is bounded on the west by Oklahoma, Kansas, and Nebraska; on the north by Iowa; on the east by Illinois, Kentucky, and Tennessee; and on the south by Arkansas. The state has four main land regions: the Dissected Till Plains, the Osage Plains, the Ozark Plateau, and the Mississippi Alluvial Plain.

The Dissected Till Plains are located in the north, just above the Missouri River. During the Ice Age, these lands were covered by glaciers that left a deep deposit of fertile soil, well watered by numerous streams.

The Osage Plains form a triangular section in the west central part of Missouri. The land here is flat, with an occasional low hill.

The Ozark Plateau is a large area extending south from the Dissected Till Plains and the Osage Plains. This is higher country, with forested hills and small mountains. It is a scenic region, with many caves, large springs, and lakes. In addition to dairy and poultry farms, there are corn, oat, sorghum, fruit, and wheat farms. Some of the region's natural resources are coal, clay, zinc, lead, marble, granite, iron ore, and limestone.

The Mississippi Alluvial Plain covers the southeastern tip of the state. The area was once a swamp, but it has been drained and the silt-rich soil is unusually fertile. This "Boot Heel," as the southern plain is called, produces cotton, corn, soybeans, and fruit.

The most important rivers in the state are the Mississippi and the Missouri, which are the nation's longest rivers. The largest lake in the state is the man-made Lake of the Ozarks, a popular recreation center of 60,000 acres with a shoreline of more than 1,300 miles.

Missouri's size and position account for a wide range of climate and temperature, with the average annual temperature at 50 degrees Fahrenheit in the northwest, 60 degrees F. in the southeast. Rainfall and other forms of precipitation average from 48 inches per year in the southeast to 32 inches in the northwest.

The History

When the first European explorers arrived in the 17th century, a number of Indian tribes occupied the region's hills and plains. In east-central Missouri there were the Missouri Indians. To the south and west were the Osage, and in the north were the Fox, the Sauk, and others.

Like many parts of the Midwest, Missouri was first explored by the French. In 1673 Father Jacques Marquette and Louis Joliet descended the Mississippi and became the first non-Indians to see the mouth of the Missouri River. Another French explorer, Robert Cavelier, known as La Salle, voyaged down the Mississippi in 1682 and claimed the Mississippi Valley for France. He named the region Louisiana, for King Louis XIV.

French trappers and fur traders began establishing trading posts along the Mississippi, and French missionaries came to spread Christianity among the Indians. About 1700 some of these missionaries founded the first non-Indian settlement in Missouri—the Mission of St. Francis Xavier, near present-day St. Louis, which was soon abandoned because of the unhealthful swamps nearby. A permanent settlement was established in 1735, at Ste. Genevieve on the Mississippi River, where lead had been discovered some years before. In 1764 St. Louis, several miles to the north, was founded by Pierre Laclède Liguest and René Auguste Chouteau. St. Louis was originally a base for fur-trading operations, which were the state's most important industry for decades to come.

France gave up its territory west of the Mississippi to Spain in 1762, and the Spanish government encouraged American settlers to come into the region. One of these pioneers from the East was Daniel Boone, the legendary frontiersman. The Spanish granted him some 800 acres of land in what is now St. Charles County and eventually appointed him a judge.

President Thomas Jefferson bought the vast Louisiana Territory from Napoleon Bonaparte, emperor of France, in 1803. Much of this land was unexplored, and Jefferson called on the surveying skills of Meriwether Lewis and William Clark. Their expedition left St. Louis in 1804 and mapped the Northwest in to the Pacific Ocean before returning in 1806.

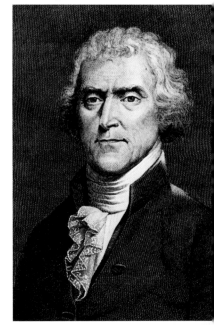

A view of St. Louis during the 1840s, when the city prospered by selling supplies to pioneers who planned to forge West.

The Gateway Arch in St. Louis, the city's best-known landmark, is a majestic 630-feet-high stainless-steel monument to westward expansion.

By 1800 Napoleon Bonaparte had become the ruler of France, and had forced Spain to return the lands west of the Mississippi. Napoleon then sold this vast region—an area three times greater than that of the original 13 colonies—to the United States in the Louisiana Purchase of 1803. When Missouri became part of the United States that year, its settlements became the staging ground for western expansion all the way to the Pacific Ocean. The expedition of Meriwether Lewis and William Clark began and ended in Missouri in 1804–1806.

The Missouri Territory was organized in 1812. In 1818 Missouri requested admission to the Union, but Congress delayed action during a national debate that lasted for several years, because many Missourians were slave owners. At the time, there were exactly as many slave states as free states, and the admission of Missouri as a slave state would upset the balance in the Senate. The result was the Missouri Compromise of 1820, in which Maine was to be admitted as a free state and Missouri as a slave state, with the proviso that slavery would not be permitted in any other state formed from the Louisiana Purchase north of Missouri's southern boundary. Missouri entered the Union in 1821 as the 24th state.

Both the Santa Fe and Oregon Trails originated in Independence, and from the 1840s St. Louis grew wealthy outfitting wagon trains for the trek west. Later, great cattle herds would be driven into Missouri from the Southwest, destined for the stockyards of Kansas City.

In 1857 fresh controversy on the slavery issue broke out when the U.S. Supreme Court issued the Dred Scott Decision. It decreed that Scott, a Missouri slave, had no rights of citizenship because he was merely property, and that state laws banning slavery were unconstitutional in depriving persons of their property without due process of law.

On the eve of the Civil War in 1861, Missouri delegates voted to remain in the Union, but when hostilities broke out, Governor Claiborne F. Jackson refused to send troops. The state militia clashed

with Union soldiers at Boonville in July 1861, and federal forces took control of northern Missouri. Governor Jackson and his troops reorganized and fought the Union soldiers again, this time at Wilson's Creek. The militia won the bloody battle, but Missouri was still torn by internal dissension about whether it should formally secede from the Union. In October 1861, the legislature voted to join the Confederacy, but there were not enough members present to give this decision the force of law. Confederate General Sterling Price tried to gain control of Missouri, but was defeated at Westport, a part of present-day Kansas City, in 1864. Throughout the Civil War, bands of Union and Confederate raiders clashed in the state, destroying life and property.

St. Louis and Kansas City became increasingly important transportation centers after the war ended in 1865, and the economy of the state flourished. The resources of Missouri were important to the armed forces during World War I, but the Great Depression of the 1930s interrupted this growth, as many mines and factories closed down and agricultural prices dropped. Federal and state programs were set up to provide relief and recovery. World War II accelerated the development of new industries between 1941 and 1945. Food processing, uranium and iron mining, chemicals, and electronics have diversified Missouri's economy, while agriculture remains important to the state. Missouri's cities have begun to specialize in particular industries. For example, St. Louis has become a center of airplane, missile, and space vehicle manufacturing.

Education

The first school in Missouri, an elementary school in St. Louis, was established in 1774. The state system of public education was created in 1839. By the time Missouri was admitted to the Union, in 1821, there were two institutions of higher education in the territory—

The Pony Express was a network of relay stations by which rugged young men carried the mail on horseback through the dangerous territories of the sparsely settled West. Missouri's position as the "gateway to the West resulted in the selection of St. Joseph as the starting point for Pony Express riders who raced to Sacramento, California, during 1860. The service was replaced by a transcontinental telegraph system in 1861.

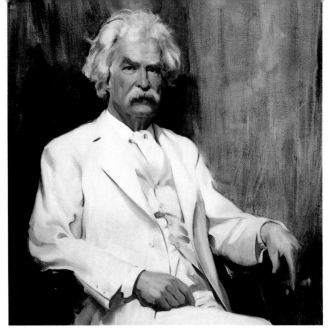

Above:
Mark Twain, born Samuel Clemens in Florida in 1835, grew up in Hannibal to become one of America's most prominent and colorful writers. His life on and near the Mississippi River is reflected in such classics as *The Adventures of Huckleberry Finn.*

Above right:
Harry S. Truman, the 33rd president of the United States, was born in Lamar. As vice-president, he succeeded Franklin D. Roosevelt, who died in office during World War II. Truman authorized the use of atomic bombs against Hiroshima and Nagasaki, Japan, to force the Japanese surrender of September 2, 1945.

Cardinal Glennon College and Saint Louis University—both founded in 1818. Only 40 years after statehood, there were nine more colleges and universities in the state. Prior to 1954, segregation by race in school attendance was required by the state constitution. By 1980 approximately 35 percent of Missouri's black pupils attended schools with a majority of white pupils and about 32 percent attended all-black schools.

The People

About 68 percent of the people in Missouri live in cities and towns, including St. Louis, Kansas City, Springfield, and St. Joseph. More than 98 percent of the residents of the state were born in the United States. Most of them had Czech, English, French, German, Irish, Italian, Polish, or Swiss ancestors. More than half of Missourians are Protestant, primarily Baptists, Disciples of Christ, Episcopalians, Lutherans, Methodists, Presbyterians, and members of the United Church of Christ. About one in six Missourians is Roman Catholic.

Famous People

Many famous people were born in the state of Missouri. Here are a few:

Ed Asner b. 1929, Kansas City. Television actor: *The Mary Tyler Moore Show, Lou Grant*

Josephine Baker 1906-75, St. Louis. Singer and dancer

Thomas Hart Benton 1889-1975, Neosho. Painter and muralist

Yogi Berra b. 1925, St. Louis. Hall of Fame baseball player

Bill Bradley b. 1943, Crystal City. Senate leader and basketball player

Omar N. Bradley 1893-1981, Clark. World War II general

Grace Bumbry b. 1937, St. Louis. Operatic mezzo-soprano

Martha Jane "Calamity Jane" Canary Burk 1852?-1903, Princeton. Frontier figure

George Washington Carver 1861-1943, near Diamond Grove. Chemist

Dale Carnegie 1888-1935, Maryville. Author and teacher of public speaking

Walter Cronkite, Jr. b. 1916, St. Joseph. Television news anchorman

Winston Churchill 1871-1947, St. Louis. Novelist: *Richard Carvel; The Crossing*

Samuel Longhorne "Mark Twain" Clemens 1835-1910, Florida. Novelist: *Tom Sawyer*

Thomas Stearns "T.S." Eliot 1888-1965, St. Louis. Poet: "The Wasteland"

Eugene Field 1850-95, St. Louis. Poet: "Little Boy Blue"

Dick Gregory b. 1932, St. Louis. Comedian, political activist, and nutritionist

Jean Harlow 1911-37, Kansas City. Film actress: *Hell's Angels, Saratoga*

Coleman Hawkins 1904-69, St. Joseph. Jazz saxophonist

George Hearst 1820-91, near Sullivan. Businessman and public official

Cal Hubbard 1900-77, Keytesville. Hall of Fame baseball umpire and Hall of Fame football player

Carl Hubbell 1903-88, Carthage. Hall of Fame baseball pitcher

Edwin P. Hubble 1889-1953, Marshfield. Astronomer

Langston Hughes 1902-67, Joplin. Poet: *The Weary Blues*

John Huston 1906-87, Nevada. Film director

Writer Langston Hughes was born in Joplin. His work, including the play *Mulatto* (1935), focused attention on racial problems in the United States.

Jesse James 1847-82, near Centerville. Outlaw

Marianne Moore 1887-1972, Kirkwood. Pulitzer Prize-winning poet: *Collected Poems, Observations*

Geraldine Page 1924-87, Kirksville. Academy Award-winning actress: *The Trip to Bountiful*

J. C. Penney 1875-1971, Hamilton. Merchant

John J. Pershing 1860-1948, near Laclede. World War I general

Vincent Price 1911-93, St. Louis. Film actor: *Laura; Theatre of Blood*

Ginger Rogers b. 1911, Independence. Academy Award-winning actress: *Kitty Foyle, Top Hat*

Casey Stengel 1890-1975, Kansas City. Hall of Fame baseball manager

Sara Teasdale 1884-1933, St. Louis. Pulitzer Prize-winning poet: *Love Songs*

Calvin Trillin b. 1935, Kansas City. Newspaper columnist

Harry S. Truman 1884-1972, Lamar. Thirty-third President of the United States

Dick Van Dyke b. 1925, West Plains. Television actor: *The Dick Van Dyke Show*

Tom Watson b. 1949, Kansas City. Champion golfer

Earl Weaver b. 1930, St. Louis. Baseball manager

Roy Wilkins 1901-81, St. Louis. Civil rights leader

Colleges and Universities
There are many colleges and universities in Missouri. Here are the more prominent, with their locations, dates of founding, and enrollments.

Central Missouri State University, Warrensburg, 1871, 11,631

Lincoln University, Jefferson City, 1866, 4,031

Lindenwood College, St. Charles, 1827, 2,825

Maryville University of Saint Louis, 1872, 3,722

Missouri Southern State College, Joplin, 1937, 5,640

Missouri Western State College, St. Joseph, 1915, 5,093

Northeast Missouri State University, Kirksville, 1867, 5,941

Northwest Missouri State University, Maryville, 1905, 5,865

Rockhurst College, Kansas City, 1910, 2,702

Saint Louis University, St. Louis, 1818, 11,747

Southeast Missouri State University, Cape Girardeau, 1873, 8,704

Southwest Missouri State University, Springfield, 1905, 19,002

Stephens College, Columbia, 1833, 1,045

University of Missouri, Columbia, 1839, 23,346; Kansas City, 1929, 10,489; Rolla, 1870, 5,657; St. Louis, 1963, 11,774

Washington University, St. Louis, 1853, 9,429

Webster University, St. Louis, 1915, 9,699

William Jewell College, Liberty, 1849, 1,384

Where To Get More Information
Chamber of Commerce 400 East High Street, P.O. Box 149
Jefferson City, MO 65101
or call, 1-800-877-1234

Oklahoma

   The state seal of Oklahoma, adopted in 1907, is circular. In the center is a five-pointed star, representing the Five Civilized Tribes of Indians that settled the territory. In the center of the star is the old territorial seal. The upper left point of the star contains the ancient seal of the Cherokee Nation; the top point, the seal of the Chickasaw Nation; the upper right point, the seal of the Choctaw Nation; the lower right point, the seal of the Seminole Nation; and the lower left point, the seal of the Creek Nation. Surrounding the star and between the points are 45 small stars, in groups of nine, representing the states already in the Union when Oklahoma entered as the 46th state. Around the edge of the seal is printed "Great Seal of the State of Oklahoma" and "1907," the year of the state's admission.

OKLAHOMA
At a Glance

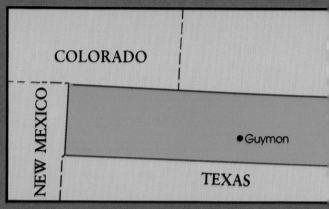

COLORADO

NEW MEXICO

• Guymon

TEXAS

Capital: Oklahoma City

Major Industries: Oil-field machinery, petroleum, agriculture

Major Crops: Wheat, cotton, sorghum, peanuts, hay, soybeans

State Flag

Size: 69,919 square miles (18th largest)
Population: 3,212,198 (28th largest)

State Flower: Mistletoe
State Bird: Scissortailed Flycatcher

State Flag
Oklahoma's state flag is blue and contains a circular rawhide shield of an Indian warrior. On the shield are six crosses, and the bottom is fringed with seven eagle feathers. Placed upon the shield are an olive branch and an Indian peace pipe. Underneath is the word "Oklahoma." The flag was adopted in 1925.

State Salute to the Flag
In 1982, a salute to the state flag was selected: "I salute the flag of the State of Oklahoma. Its symbols of peace unite all people."

The view from atop Mount Scott in the Wichita Mountain National Wildlife Refuge in Lawton.

State Capital

The capital of Oklahoma was Guthrie from 1890 until 1910. Oklahoma City was named the capital in 1910.

State Motto

Labor Omnia Vincit, which translates from the Latin as Labor conquers all things.

State Name and Nicknames

The word Oklahoma comes from two Choctaw Indian words. *Okla* means "person," and *humma* means "red." Therefore, Oklahoma means "red person."

Oklahoma is called the *Sooner State* or *Boomer's Paradise*. Both of these refer to the opening of the territory in 1889. Sooners were those who illegally came into the territory to stake claims before the appointed hour. Boomers were those who came in legally to settle the new land.

State Flower

In 1893, mistletoe, *Phoradendron serotinum*, was adopted as state flower.

State Tree

Selected in 1937, the redbud tree, *Cercis canadensis*, is the state tree of Oklahoma.

State Bird

The scissortailed flycatcher, *Muscivora forticata*, was named state bird in 1951.

State Animal

The American buffalo, *Bison americanus*, was selected as state animal in 1972.

State Colors

Green and white have been the state colors since 1915.

State Fish

The white bass, *Morone chrysops*, was adopted as state fish in 1974.

State Grass

In 1972, Indian grass, *Sorghastrum nutans*, became the state grass.

State Poem

"Howdy Folks," by David Randolph Milsten, was selected in 1973.

State Reptile

Adopted in 1969, the collared lizard, *Crotophytus*, is the state reptile.

State Rock

Barite rose was named state rock in 1968.

State Songs

Oklahoma has had two state songs. From 1935 to 1953, it was "Oklahoma (A Toast)," by Harriet Parker Camden. In 1953, the present state song was substituted. It is "Oklahoma," with words by Oscar Hammerstein II and music by Richard Rodgers.

Population

The population of Oklahoma in 1992 was 3,212,198, making it the 28th most populous state. There are 45 persons per square mile.

Industries

The principal industries of the state of Oklahoma are mineral and energy exploration and production, printing and publishing, and agriculture. The chief manufactured products are nonelectrical machinery, fabricated metal products, and petroleum. Oklahoma's extensive mineral resources include petroleum, natural gas, and coal. These represent over 95 percent of the value of the state's mineral production.

Agriculture

The chief crops of the state are wheat, hay, peanuts, grain sorghum, soybeans, corn, pecans, oats, barley, and rye. Oklahoma is also a livestock state, and there are estimated to be some 5.2 million cattle, 215,000 hogs and pigs, 135,000 sheep, and 4.75 million poultry on its farms. Pine, oak, and hickory trees are harvested. Crushed stone, cement, sand, and gravel are important mineral resources.

Government

The governor is elected to a four-year term, as are the lieutenant governor, attorney general, treasurer, auditor, and superintendent of public instruction. The state legislature consists of a senate of 48 members and a house of representatives of 101 members. Senators serve four-year terms and representatives serve two-year terms. Each senator and representative is elected from a different district. The most recent state constitution was adopted in 1907. In addition to its two U.S. senators, Oklahoma has six representatives in the U.S. House of Representatives. The state has eight votes in the electoral college.

Sports

Sports, especially on the collegiate level, have always been important in Oklahoma. It, along with Iowa, is a wrestling hotbed. In basketball, Oklahoma A & M won the NCAA championship (1945, 1946). In football, Oklahoma A & M, Tulsa, and the University of Oklahoma have won numerous bowl games. The NCAA baseball championship has been won by the University of Oklahoma (1951) and

Oklahoma State University (1959).

Major Cities

Lawton (population 80,561). Like the state capital and a number of other cities in Oklahoma, Lawton was founded one day in August 1901. Lawton is a trading center for agricultural products and underwent a massive expansion in 1930 when the nearby artillery and missile base, Fort Sill Military Reservation, was constructed.
Things to see in Lawton:
Military museum, Museum of the Great Plains, grave of

The Will Rogers Memorial in Claremore is a stone ranch house with exhibits about the much loved cowboy humorist and memorabilia of Indian and pioneer days.

Indian City, U.S.A, located near Anadarko, displays Plains Indian settlements of the early 1800s.

Geronimo, Apache Prisoner of War Cemetery, Medicine Bluffs, and approximately 50 other historic sites.

Oklahoma City (population 444,719). Founded in 1889, the capital city was empty prairie on the morning of April 22, the day of the Great Land Run of 1889, when a pistol shot sent 10,000 settlers scrambling to stake their claim. The most populous city in Oklahoma, this is the third largest city in the nation in land area (630 square miles).

It is the primary market for the Oklahoma livestock industry. Its stockyards are the largest stocker and feeder cattle market in the world, handling over 1 million head of livestock per year. In addition, Oklahoma is a prime petroleum producer, a site of aircraft manufacturing and repair, as well as a center of meat packing, grain milling, and cotton processing.

Things to see in Oklahoma City:
State Capitol, State Museum of History, Oklahoma Art Center, ArtsPlace, International Photography Hall of Fame and Museum, Kirkpatrick Planetarium, OMNIPLEX, Harn Homestead and 1889er Museum, 45th Infantry Division Museum, National Softball Hall of Fame and Museum, National Cowboy Hall of Fame and Western Heritage Center, Oklahoma City Zoo, Aquaticus, Oklahoma Firefighters Museum, Oklahoma Museum of Art, Oklahoma Heritage Center, Oklahoma National Stock Yards, Frontier City, and White Water.

Tulsa (population 367,302). Founded in 1879, Tulsa is the "oil capital of the world." The first well was discovered in 1901. This city's name is derived from Talsi or Talasi—a branch of Creek Indians who settled at this site in 1832 after having been moved by the federal government. With over 1,000 petroleum-related firms in the Tulsa metropolitan area, it remains an oil center. In addition, aviation and aerospace are important industries that have created a diverse, well-balanced economy. The inland port at Catoosa is a home of barge shipping, and the city is a cultural and educational center.

Things to see in Tulsa:
Thomas Gilcrease Institute of American History and Art, Tulsa County Historical Society Museum, Philbrook Museum of Art, Gershon and Rebecca Fenster Museum of Jewish Art, Tulsa Zoological Park, Tulsa Garden Center, Allen Ranch Inc., and Creek Nation Council Oak Tree.

Places to Visit

The National Park service maintains two areas in the state of Oklahoma: Chickasaw National Recreation Area and Ouachita National Forest. In addition, there are 39 state recreation areas.

Anadarko: Indian City—USA. Guided tours of reconstructed villages of seven Plains Indian tribes.

Claremore: Will Rogers Birthplace. The home where the great American humorist was born.

Durant: Fort Washita. Built in 1842, it was used to protect the Five Civilized tribes from the Plains Indians.

Pawhuska: Osage Tribal Museum. The museum centering on Osage history.

Pawnee: Pawnee Bill Museum and Park. Memorabilia of the Wild West Show pioneer.

Ponca City: Pioneer Woman Museum. A pioneer home and ranch contain exhibits of pioneer family life.

Sallisaw: Sequoyah's Home. Built around 1829, this is the log cabin where the Cherokee who devised an Indian alphabet lived.

Stillwater: National Wrestling Hall of Fame. This museum is dedicated to wrestling history.

Tahlequah: Cherokee Heritage Center. Attractions include a museum and ancient village.

Events

Here are some of the many events scheduled in Oklahoma.

Sports: Great Plains Stampede Rodeo (Altus), Durant Western Days and International Rodeo Association Rodeo (Durant), Rodeo of Champions (Elk City), National Parachute Championships (Muskogee), World Championship Quarter Horse Show (Oklahoma City), Creek Nation Rodeo and Festival (Okmulgee), Heart of America Bullriding Championship (Shawnee), International Finals Rodeo (Tulsa).

Music: Tri-State Music Festival (Enid), Sanders Family Bluegrass Festival (McAlester), Oklahoma Philharmonic Orchestra (Oklahoma City), Ballet Oklahoma (Oklahoma City), Tulsa Ballet Theater (Tulsa), Tulsa Opera (Tulsa), Tulsa Philharmonic (Tulsa).

Arts and Crafts: Clinton Art Festival (Clinton), Festifall

Entertainment: Kiowa Apache Ceremonial (Anadarko), American Indian Exposition (Anadarko), Santa Fe Trail Daze Celebration (Boise City), Kiamichi Owa Chito Festival (Broken Bow), Antique Car Swap Meet (Chickasha), Will Rogers Day Celebration (Claremore), Mid-America Summerfest (Enid), Cherokee Strip Celebration (Enid), Kiamichi Owa Chito Festival of the Forest (Idabel), Indian Summer Festival (Muskogee), 89er Celebration (Norman), Festival of the Arts (Oklahoma City), Red Earth (Oklahoma City), State Fair of Oklahoma (Oklahoma City), Osage Indian Tribal Dances (Pawhuska), Indian Powwow (Pawnee), Cherokee Strip Celebration (Perry), Ponca Indian Powwow (Ponca City), Sac and Fox Powwow (Shawnee), Cherokee National Holiday (Tahlequah), Tulsa Charity Horse Show (Tulsa), Tulsa Indian Powwow (Tulsa), Tulsa State Fair (Tulsa).

Tours: Dogwood Tours (Tahlequah).

Theater: The Oklahoma Shakespearean Festival (Durant), Rupel Jones Theater (Norman), Civic Center Music Hall (Oklahoma City), Lyric Theatre (Oklahoma City), "Trail of Tears" (Tahlequah).

The vast plains in Oklahoma provide an ideal environment for raising cattle. This prime land attracted thousands of homesteaders, or "Boomers," when it was opened to white settlement in 1889. One area settled then, Oklahoma City, has since grown into the largest cattle market in the world.

The Ouachita National Forest is part of the Ouachita Mountain Range, in southeastern Oklahoma. This heavily wooded region supplies the state's lumber industry.

The Land and the Climate

Oklahoma is bounded on the west by New Mexico and Texas, on the north by Colorado and Kansas, on the east by Missouri and Arkansas, and on the south by Texas. The state has 10 main land regions. They are the Ozark Plateau, the Prairie Plains, the Ouachita Mountains, the Sandstone Hills, the Arbuckle Mountains, the Wichita Mountains, the Red River Region, the Red Beds Plains, the Gypsum Hills, and the High Plains.

The Ozark Plateau is located in northeastern Oklahoma and extends into Missouri and Arkansas. It is a hilly region with many streams and river valleys. Beef cattle, oats, corn, and soybeans are raised here.

The Prairie Plains are west and south of the Ozark Plateau. This is an important cattle-ranching area, and also a region of vegetable crops. Most of the state's coal and much of its oil are found in this region.

The Ouachita Mountains are located in southeastern Oklahoma on the Arkansas border. These sandstone ridges divided by narrow valleys are the roughest land surface in the state. The most important industry here is lumbering.

The Sandstone Hills extend from the Kansas border south to the Red River. This is a region of low hills, partially covered with forests

Much of eastern Oklahoma is characterized by plateaus and low mountains.

of blackjack and post oak. The region has important petroleum reserves and contains dairy, hog, and fruit farms.

The Arbuckle Mountains form a small wedge in south-central Oklahoma. These hills were once mighty mountains, now worn down by erosion to form a rocky landscape that is largely unsuitable for agriculture.

The granite peaks of the Wichita Mountains rise over a small section of southwestern Oklahoma. Little farming is done here; most of the area lies within the Fort Sill military reservation and a federal wildlife refuge watered by numerous streams.

The Red River Region consists of gently rolling prairies and wooded land in southeastern Oklahoma, on the Texas border. Cotton, peanuts, corn, and vegetables are grown in the sandy soil of this fertile area.

The Red Beds Plains, named for the soft red sandstone and shale beneath them, form a strip down the central part of Oklahoma from Kansas to Texas. Livestock, cotton, and wheat are raised here.

The Gypsum Hills are located west of the Red Bed Plains and rise to 200 feet above sea level. Some sheep, cattle, and wheat are raised here.

The High Plains comprise an area of level grassland in the northwest, including the Panhandle region. The land rises from about 2,000 feet in the eastern section to 4,978 feet at Black Mesa, the highest point in the state. This westernmost section of Oklahoma supports sorghum, broomcorn, wheat, and cattle.

The main river systems in Oklahoma are the Red and the Arkansas. The state has about 100 small natural lakes and more than 200 man-made lakes.

The weather in Oklahoma is primarily warm and dry—typical of the south-central states. July temperatures climb to 90 degrees Fahrenheit and above, with an average of 83 degrees F. In January the average temperature is around 40 degrees F. The state receives up to 25 inches of snow per year in the northern Panhandle, with as little as 2 inches falling in the southeast. Rainfall is heaviest in southeastern Oklahoma.

The Quartz Mountains belong to the Wichita chain, in southwestern Oklahoma, where underlying granite makes much of the land unsuitable for farming.

85

A Comanche treks across Oklahoma's snowy plains on horseback. The Comanche were among the many Indian tribes who originally inhabited the region.

This "ghost dance shirt," made by Pawnee Indians native to Oklahoma, was worn by elders of the tribe during sacred ceremonies.

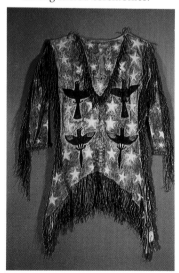

The History

The first inhabitants of what is now Oklahoma were Plains Indians, whose migratory way of life was dependent upon the great buffalo herds that roamed the Western prairies. Tribes encountered by European explorers included the Arapaho, Caddo, Cheyenne, Comanche, Kiowa, Osage, Pawnee, and Wichita.

The first Europeans to enter the Oklahoma area were Francisco Vásquez de Coronado and his men, who arrived in 1541. Another band of Spanish explorers, led by Hernando de Soto, also came into the region in search of the legendary Seven Cities of Cibola. The Spanish failed to find the gold they sought, and left the Indians undisturbed until the late 17th century. Then French fur traders and explorers passed through in the wake of the French explorer Robert Cavelier, known as La Salle, who had claimed all the land drained by the Mississippi River for his country in 1682.

What is now Oklahoma became United States territory with the Louisiana Purchase of 1803. Subdivisions of the vast Louisiana Territory resulted in Oklahoma's becoming part of the Missouri

Territory and then of the Arkansas Territory. The region's first large-scale settlements were made in the 1820s by Choctaw and Chickasaw Indians. In the 1830s they were pushed by federal authorities to leave their traditional homes and move farther west so that white settlers could move into them. The Indians established permanent villages, farmed, set up schools and law courts of their own, and created a written version of their language. In 1859 they joined with the Cherokee, Creek, and Seminole to form a federation known as the Five Civilized Tribes because they had adopted many

Fur trader and pioneer Pierre Chouteau led an Osage Indian band into present-day Oklahoma and established the first trading post near Salina in 1802.

Millions of Texas cattle were driven along the Chisholm Trail, between the Rio Grande and Abilene, Kansas, during the 1860s. The trail passed through central Oklahoma, and "cow towns" and cities flourished along the route.

customs of the European and American settlers. The Oklahoma area was designated Indian Territory, with a portion assigned to each of these five tribes, which were to be self-governing tribal nations within their assigned territories.

Between 1830 and 1846, 20,000 Creeks from Georgia and Alabama, 5,000 Choctaws from Mississippi and Louisiana, 4,000 Chickasaws from Mississippi, and 3,000 Seminoles from Florida were forced into this area. In 1838 and 1839, some 16,000 Cherokees were marched west from their lands in North Carolina, Tennessee, and Georgia by troops under the command of General Winfield Scott. About one-fourth of those forced west over this "Trail of Tears" died en route of hunger, disease, cold, and exhaustion.

After the Civil War of 1861–1865, homesteaders were pushing westward in ever greater numbers. For a time the government refused to move the Indians and punished white trespassers, but eventually the treaty that had promised the Indians their lands for "as long as grass shall grow and rivers run" was broken. Nearby areas were filling up with settlers eager to encroach upon the Indian reservations. During the 1870s and 1880s, homesteaders called "Boomers" urged the government to open Indian Territory to white settlement. The government yielded and bought more than 3,000,000 acres from the Creek and Seminole tribes. Some 1,900,000 acres in central Oklahoma were declared open for settlement as of high noon of April 22, 1889. Thousands of homesteaders waited on the border until a pistol was fired to signify that the territory was open for settlement, then stampeded into the area to choose the best sites for towns and farms. (Those who entered the region before the land rush officially began were called "Sooners"—hence the state's nickname.) Some 50,000 people moved into Oklahoma on the first day. Subsequent "runs" and lotteries brought additional thousands, especially after the Cherokee Outlet was opened to white settlement in 1893.

Twin Territories were created in 1890, when maps showed two separate entities: Indian Territory and Oklahoma Territory. As

additional settlers arrived, federal commissioners began to prepare the population for statehood. The Indian nations were dissolved, and what remained of the treaty lands were allotted to individual Indians rather than to their tribes. Indian efforts to create a separate state called Sequoyah were defeated, and the combined Twin Territories became the 46th state in 1907.

In the early 1920s, numerous governors and other state officials were impeached on charges of corruption. During the territorial period, farming had developed rapidly and oil had been discovered. Expansion continued until the 1920s, when drought and a drop in farm prices brought economic problems, worsened by the Great Depression of the 1930s. Thousands of farmers left their land to become migrant "Okies," as they were called, when prolonged heat and high winds created the Dust Bowl.

Approximately 200,000 Oklahomans served during World War II. Oklahoma's crops, fuel, and livestock were needed for the war effort, and growth resumed. Exploration for petroleum and natural gas brought new discoveries. In the 1950s, Oklahoma began to manufacture electronic equipment, plastics, and textiles to diversify the economy. Today, improved irrigation and water power have benefited both farming and industry.

A view of Oklahoma City in 1890, the year in which Congress passed an act establishing the Oklahoma Territory in the western part of the state. Eastern Oklahoma had been designated Indian Territory in 1825.

Attorney and diplomat Patrick J. Hurley was born to a Choctaw family in Indian Territory in 1883. He represented the Choctaw Nation in Washington, D.C., served as secretary of war under President Herbert Hoover, and represented President Franklin D. Roosevelt in dealings with the Allies during World War II.

Education

The first Oklahoma schools were founded by missionaries to educate Indian children in the 1820s. The territorial legislature provided for public education for white children in 1890. In that year a teacher-training college was opened and later became known as the Central State University of Edmond. In 1892 an agricultural and mechanical college opened in Stillwater and later became known as Oklahoma State University. By 1907, 10 colleges and universities were operating in the newly created state.

Oklahoma City, the state's capital, is also its largest city, with a population of more than 400,000.

The People

More than 67 percent of the people in Oklahoma live in Oklahoma City, Tulsa, and other cities and towns. More than 95 percent of them were born in the United States; almost 6 percent of them are American Indians. The largest religious groups in the state are the Baptists, Episcopalians, Methodists, and Presbyterians.

Humorist, cowboy, actor, and news commentator Will Rogers was born in 1879 in Oologah, Indian Territory, to a family of mixed Irish and Cherokee ancestry. He is remembered as a warm, down-to-earth observer of the American scene.

Famous People

Many famous people were born in the state of Oklahoma. Here are a few:

Carl Bert Albert b. 1908, McAlester. Public official and speaker of the U.S. House of Representatives

Johnny Bench b. 1947, Oklahoma City. Hall of Fame baseball player

John Berryman 1914-72, McAlester. Pulitzer Prize-winning poet: *77 Dream Songs*

Acee Blue Eagle 1910-59, near Anadarka. Artist

Gordon Cooper b. 1927, Shawnee. Astronaut

Blake Edwards b. 1922, Tulsa. Director: ''Pink Panther'' films and *Victor/Victoria*

Ralph Ellison 1914-94, Oklahoma City. Novelist: *Invisible Man*

Woodrow Wilson ''Woody'' Guthrie 1912-67, Okemah. Folk singer and composer

Roy Harris 1898-1979, Lincoln County. Composer: *When Johnny Comes Marching Home*

Paul Harvey b. 1918, Tulsa. Radio commentator

Van Heflin 1910-71, Walters. Academy Award-winning actor: *Johnny Eager, Shane*

Patrick Jay Hurley 1883-1963, Indian territory. Diplomat

Karl Guthe Jansky 1905-50, Norman. Engineer who discovered radio waves from space

Robert Samuel Kerr 1896-1963, Ada. Political figure

Jeanne Kirkpatrick b. 1926, Duncan. U.S. ambassador to the United Nations

Mickey Mantle b. 1931, Spavinaw. Hall of Fame baseball player

Bill Moyers b. 1934, Hugo. Television commentator

James A. Pike 1913-69, Oklahoma City. Episcopal bishop

Tony Randall b. 1920, Tulsa. Actor: *The Odd Couple*

Oral Roberts b. 1918, Ada. Evangelist

Will Rogers 1879-1935, near Oologah. Humorist

Willie Stargell b. 1940, Earlsboro. Hall of Fame baseball player

Gordon Cooper was the first American to spend a day in space when he orbited the earth 22 times on May 15, 1963.

Jim Thorpe 1887-1953, Prague. Hall of Fame football player and Olympic gold medal winner

Colleges and Universities
There are many colleges and universities in Oklahoma. Here are the more prominent, with their locations, dates of founding, and enrollments.

Northeastern State University, Tahlequah, 1846, 9,023

Northwestern Oklahoma State University, Alva, 1897, 2,106

Oklahoma City University, Oklahoma City, 1904, 4,450

Oklahoma State University of Agriculture and Applied Science, Stillwater, 1890, 19,477

Oral Roberts University, Tulsa, 1963, 4,054

Southeastern Oklahoma State University, Durant, 1909, 4,109

Southwestern Oklahoma State University, Weatherford, 1901, 4,953

University of Oklahoma, Norman, 1890, 20,015

University of Tulsa, Tulsa, 1894, 4,922

Where To Get More Information

Oklahoma Tourism Department
P.O. Box 60789
Oklahoma City, OK 73146-0789
or call, 1-800-652-6552

Further Reading

General

Aylesworth, Thomas G. and Virginia L. Aylesworth. *State Reports: South Central*. New York: Chelsea House, 1992.

Arkansas

Ashmore, Harry S. *Arkansas: A History*. New York: Norton, 1984.

Bradley, Donald M. *Arkansas: Its Land and People*. Little Rock: Little Rock Museum of Science and Industry, 1980.

Carpenter, Allan. *Arkansas*, rev. ed. Chicago: Childrens Press, 1978.

Heinrichs, Ann. *America the Beautiful: Arkansas*. Chicago: Childrens Press, 1989.

Kansas

Carpenter, Allan. *Kansas*, rev. ed. Chicago: Childrens Press, 1981.

Davis, Kenneth S. *Kansas: A History*. New York: Norton, 1984.

Kent, Zachary. *America the Beautiful: Kansas*. Chicago: Childrens Press, 1991.

Richmond, Robert W. *Kansas: A Land of Contrasts*, 2nd ed. St. Louis: Forum Press, 1980.

Louisiana

Davis, Edwin A., and others. *Louisiana: The Pelican State*, rev. ed. Baton Rouge: Louisiana State University Press, 1985.

Kent, Deborah. *America the Beautiful: Louisiana*. Chicago: Childrens Press, 1988.

Taylor, Joe Gray. *Louisiana: A History*. New York: Norton, 1984.

Wall, Bennett H., and Charles E. O'Neill. *Louisiana: A History*. Arlington Heights, IL: Forum Press, 1984.

Missouri

Bailey, Bernadine. *Picture Book of Missouri*, rev. ed. Chicago: Whitman, 1974.

Carpenter, Allan. *Missouri*, rev. ed. Chicago: Childrens Press, 1974.

Fradin, Dennis B. *Missouri in Words and Pictures*. Chicago:

Childrens Press, 1980.

Meyer, Duane G. *The Heritage of Missouri*, 3rd ed. St. Louis: River City Publishers, 1982.

Parrish, William E., and others. *Missouri: The Heart of the Nation*. St. Louis: Forum Press, 1980.

Sanford, William R. and Carl R. Green. *America the Beautiful: Missouri*. Chicago: Childrens Press, 1990.

Oklahoma

Carpenter, Allan. *Oklahoma*, rev. ed. Chicago: Childrens Press, 1979.

Fradin, Dennis B. *Oklahoma in Words and Pictures*. Chicago: Childrens Press, 1981.

Gibson, Arrell M., and Victor E. Harlow. *The History of Oklahoma*. Norman, 1984.

Heinrichs, Ann. *America the Beautiful: Oklahoma*. Chicago: Childrens Press, 1989.

Morgan, Howard W., and Anne H. *Oklahoma: A History*. New York: Norton, 1984.

Numbers in italics refer to illustrations

Picture Credits

Courtesy of the Arkansas Department of Parks and Tourism: pp. 5, 7, 8-9, 11, 13, 17, 18; Courtesy of the Arkansas Department of Parks and Tourism/Robyn Horn: pp. 3 (top), 14-15, 16; Courtesy of the Arkansas Department of Parks and Tourism/Pat Pickett: p. 12; Courtesy of Fort Leavenworth: p. 30; Courtesy of the Kansas Department of Economic Development: pp. 3 (bottom), 24, 26-27, 31, 32-33, 34, 35; Courtesy of Kansas Secretary of State: p. 23; Courtesy of the Louisiana Office of Tourism: pp. 4 (top), 39, 40, 41, 42-43, 47, 48-49, 50, 53 (top); Courtesy of the Missouri Division of Tourism: pp. 4 (middle), 55, 57, 58-59, 61, 62, 64-65, 66, 68, 69; Museum of the American Indian: p. 86; Courtesy of NASA: p. 92; National Portrait Gallery: pp. 37, 70, 71; New York Public Library/Stokes Collection: pp. 34 (top), 89; Courtesy of the Oklahoma Division of Tourism/Fred W. Marvel: pp. 4 (bottom), 74, 76-77, 79, 80, 82-83, 84, 85, 90; Courtesy of Oklahoma Secretary of State: p. 73; Courtesy of Pittsburgh Steelers: p. 53 (bottom left).

Cover photos courtesy of the Arkansas Department of Parks and Tourism; Fort Leavenworth; Louisiana Office of Tourism; Missouri Division of Tourism; and the Oklahoma Division of Tourism/Fred W. Marvel.